A Brief Introduction to Holy Quraan

for the Present Day Inquisitive, *Skeptical and Argumentative Beginners of All Social Groups and Research Oriented Academicians in the World*

A Brief Introduction to Holy Quraan

for the Present Day Inquisitive, Skeptical and Argumentative Beginners of All Social Groups and Research Oriented Academicians in the World

Dr. Adhikarla S. Rao

KALPAZ

First Published, 2018

Published by

Kalpaz Publications
C-30, Satyawati Nagar,
Delhi – 110052
E-mail: kalpaz@hotmail.com
Ph.: 9212142040

Printed at: G. Print Process, Delhi

Cataloging in Publication Data—DK
Courtesy: D.K. Agencies (P) Ltd. <docinfo@dkagencies.com>

Rao, Adhikarla S., author.
A brief introduction to Holy Quraan : for the present day inquisitive, skeptical and argumentative beginners of all social groups and research oriented academicians in the world / Dr. Adhikarla S. Rao.
pages cm
ISBN 9789386397355 (HB)

1. Qur' an—basics/prescriptions, appraisal, etc. I. Title.

LCC BP130.4.R36 2018 | DDC 297.1226 23

Contents

Foreword

This book is a valuable addition to the list of books on comparative philosophy, religion, social practices and culture. I admire the author Dr A. S. Rao for bringing together so many important details without any offense or bias and with the noble intention of promoting mutual understanding among people across the country and the globe. As I myself have been actively involved for decades in promoting values and harmony I can really feel the strength of the book.

I have therefore no hesitation in acknowledging the utility of the book by Dr Rao to a wide range of readers as mentioned in the apt title of the book. I feel that the book is a 'good read' for all.

Professor Dr P. Tauro Ph.D (Wisc)
Ex Professor of Eminence &
Dean Postgraduate Studies,
HAU, Hisar 125004 (Haryana)

Acknowledgement

I express my wholehearted thanks to Dr Y. Satyanarayana, Professor, Department of English, Anwarul Uloom College, Hyderabad—500001, Telangana, who is well versed in Urdu, Persian and Comparative Literature. Conversations with him over a long period of time were very valuable to me.

Preface

An earnest plea to the readers. Initially I thought I would just confine myself to the first part of the title of the book- and accordingly keep the title too-, but I got some other thoughts flowing into and disturbing my mind. I thought if I just confine myself to some prescriptions in Quraan, the readers both within the country and across the world are very likely to get an impression that I am too naive about so many things and did not take any pains to know and write keeping several others viewpoints in mind. This feeling was very heavy on my mind. Hence, I had to include several other aspects/points. Some of the points mentioned pave the way for writing some more books by research oriented academicians.

In the process of my writing, I have gone through three English versions of Quraans viz. (a) The Holy Quraan, English Translation by Mohd. Marmaduke Picthall, 1978, Islamic Book Service, New Delhi, India; (b) The Holy Quraan, English Translation of the meanings and commentary; Al-Madinah Al-Munawarah, The Ministry of Hajj and Endowments, Mecca, 2011; (c) Noble Quran: Interpretation of the meanings of Noble Quran in the English language. Muhammad Muhsin Khan and Muhammad Taqi-ud-Din Al-Hilali, 1996, Darussalam, Riyadh etc and two more books; (d) Karren Armstrong (1993)-A History of God-Vintage Books, London and (e) History of Arabs by Philip. K. Hitti 1970 and its revised tenth edition-2002 with the copy right of Walid Khalidi, Palgrave Macmillan, USA, UK etc. My writing is based exclusively on the English translations. Of course, Google was consulted but Google—as for many other subjects for that matter—is an ocean and my life time may not be sufficient to go through all the sites. Further information on different sites of Google can be different. Hence, I can only say a few sites were browsed but not swayed away by these. Only few points worthwhile have been mentioned. While people may find each of the above Quraan useful in its own way, Picthall deserves a special mention. It gives Arabic transliterations of all the verses in the Quraan (by M. Abdul Haleem Eliyasee). So one can get easily familiarised with Arabic expressions, sounds and vocabulary. Darussalam Quraan has mentioned numerous Arabic words along with their corresponding English meanings/ explanation. The entire list of these words will give a good idea of so many important concepts/tenets in Islam and it is easy to memorise these vocabulary. These terms could have been as well given as an Index or Glossary.

Compilers of Madinah Quraan deserves lot of appreciation. They did a commendable job. A very elaborate and didactic index is given with the help of which one can understand many basic tenets of Islam.The Quraan gives a huge number of footnotes to every Surah and cumulatively they are a huge number—6310 footnotes in all. Information given in footnotes is highly valuable and scholars/clergy of all affiliations can do research on the information provided on these footnotes and write additional books. The compilers are really honest and commendable in giving even information which may be considered as embarrassing by others. Mentions many practices which were there before prophet started preaching. Footnotes cover a wide range of information. Further every Surah has an Introduction and summary. In addition the compilers have provided seven useful Appendices. Contents are well tabulated and informative. All these make this Quraan highly useful.

Further, I have included very few points from Hinduism and Bible etc and viewpoints of both ordinary and qualified public. Wherever I have given my opinions I have given them in brackets, quoting in the beginning as "Self". (Strictly speaking they are not really my opinions but are formed in me as a result of studying several books, news media and listening to several categories of people across the country and from other countries over a long period of time). Other author's statements and opinions I have given in inverted quotes/commas. For explaining what is mentioned in the Quraan, I stuck to what is there in the English translations of the original books as mentioned above.

And I must say that I have confined only to Quraan and not to any other texts which Muslims take into consideration for their reference –sunnah/hadith. As per Islam, Quraan is a divine revelation, the word of God and the absolute truth. Hence, for beginners of all social groups and research oriented academicians starting with Quraan is more convincing and desirable.

I strongly and earnestly advise everyone, irrespective of one's affiliation—more particularly the academicians and custodians of culture of all backgrounds to read Quraan and it is not a difficult task. Rather it is an easy task as it is a small book with just 6236/6238 verses. While writing the book I often felt that Prophet Muhammad should have lived for much longer time. Had he lived much longer, many details, doubts and his ideology would have been more clearly known.

Different people use different spellings for the same words. For example, Quran/Quraan/Koran; Muslim/Moslem, Madina/Medina/ Medinah; Mecca/ Makka; Surat/Surah etc. There are so many words like that. I have used spellings which I am more familiar with. As there are so many Arabic words written with different English spellings, it would be an useful exercise for bilingual professionals i.e. those who have mastery over both Arabic and English languages come together and reach a consensus on the English spellings of various Arabic words. A compilation of all this would be highly useful and should be published in the form of a book. It is a good commercial venture as well besides achieving an uniformity all over the world.

A little bit of repetitions in the text and bolding of words/sentences is made inview of the context. But I tried my best to keep the size of the text as smaller—but retaining the essence and the major basic tenets of Quraan—for an easy and fast learning and to satisfy a larger and wider audience. Any interpretation made by me, I request the readers to take in a positive sense—that it will help in clarifying a point or a situation better- and not at all with any negative sense or feelings. These will also help people of all categories of affiliations to understand Quraan better and for Muslims to know how in the present day times, even genuine people also across the world may get doubts and in turn they can accordingly give better clarifications and defence.

In the present times we have an increasing number of educated people that too in science and the present world is so different compared to the ancient times. So they naturally get so many types of doubts genuinely. But they can be genuine seekers for universal outlook and universal peace and harmony. My points also reflect the above peoples likely way of thinking. And having a proper understanding of each other across the globe will contribute towards global peace and harmony.

As a professional Biochemist I was teaching for a long time the unity or commonality among various groups of organisms—microorganism-plants-animals-humans. A biochemist finds similarities/commonalities even in such wide range of organisms. I used to tell the chemical composition of a human body which does not indicate any thing about any human related to any particular religion. Something true for all. We do not have separate medical degrees for different religions and faiths or ideologies. All social groups in a particular place study in the same medical college with the same curriculum. Our commonality we should discover and try to have an universal outlook and work for universal peace. A Hindu saying is 'sarvey jana sukhino bhavanthu" meaning, "Let all remain happy". So Live and Let Live should be our principle.

I swear that I have not become blasphemous to any religion but only tried to cater for the intentions of curious general public and qualified public in the modern era (In the title the former I have referred to as inquisitive, skeptical and argumentative. Qualified public refer to research oriented academicians. They can belong to so many different religions, regions, faiths, cults, atheists, agnostics etc. Further these people can be of different age groups, different educational status and mental maturity etc. So I have to keep a large number of heterogeneous readers while writing the book.). The author's calibre to serve such a large audience may be doubted but not the intentions in any way. I sincerely feel that my text would not only help as an easy reckoner to many but also motivate many in several academic institutions across the globe to take up important book writing and research projects. Primary aim and hope kept in mind while writing this book is that "We Should All Live in Peace and Harmony".

Before any one expresses any opinions, one should keep in mind that now it is twenty-first century -2017 and beyond. So lot of time has passed since different religions have started and the present day modern world. This time may differ from religion to religion. At the time a religion has started the social, economic, political, cultural, development of Science and Technology, availability of various goods and services, life experiences etc were so much different and accordingly they had to function. As the above conditions have considerably changed with time, gradually changes also might have come the way people function. As on today the above conditions are so different. Different denominations, different interpretations, different perspectives, etc have emerged since the time of the start of the religions. Older the religion greater will be the above. All these might have been done based on the understanding of the prevailing scholars to suit to the prevailing situations and /or the will of the ruler and /or the prevailing custodians of the society so as to suit the prevailing conditions. In the present times, the type of governance also is different in different places—Democracy, Communism, Kings, Dictatorship, Socialism etc. And accordingly the people's way of functioning would be different. How many things can be treated as absolute and how many as relative, is debatable. Since the start of a religion many generations have passed by and today we have the "nth" generation-"n" value varying from religion to religion. Science and technology has advanced tremendously and provided so many goods and services. Many countries have become extremely rich, have an excellent modern infrastructure, access to modern goods and services. Nature of warfare, communications, transport, healthcare, attitudes, international relations etc all have changed with so many people belonging to all religions and regions of the world. Now we talk about "Global village", that is the entire globe is open and all people can get exposed to it in so many ways both physically and otherwise. The world -culture and peoples way of life has drastically changed at so many places. Further, before I express other authors or my views on God/Religion/news media facts etc, let me tell that before Jesus Christ (approximately 2000 years back) and before Prophet Muhammad (born 570 and attained prophethood in 610) there were no Christians or Muslims on the globe. But today they form the largest and the second largest population in the world! So one cannot dismiss something highly significantly positive and superiority about the founders of and the followers of these religions and significantly negative in the societies of those who have got converted into the above religions. Something for the Academicians/Scholars/philosophers all over the world to analyse this with the ultimate objective of arriving at Universal Peace. The third Abrahamic religion Judaism though much older to the above, Jews constitute only a tiny minority in the world.

Another significant development over a period of time, in spite of so many religions is, as on today atheists/agnostics and related groups (termed as "Unaffiliated" in the world census) form the third largest population in the world. And their number is likely to increase further. (though a few say it may decrease slightly). Many of these atheists were once upon a time were Christians or Hindus etc and in countries like Japan and China they were following Shintoism, Buddhism, Confucianism etc. Though they are unaffiliated they must be having some philosophy to function. For a long time unaffiliated group was a tiny number. They have replaced Hindus from the third group i.e. as the third largest over a period of time.

Hindus, though they are considered as the fourth largest population as on today, there are no predominantly Hindu countries the way we have countries with Christianity and Islam as official state religion, across the world. It is primarily because of one country–India—whose population being very large, Hindus have become the fourth largest population in the world. Nepal's contribution is small. And still smaller the contribution, population of Hindus scattered all over the globe. However, both these countries are not referred to as Hindu countries—the way we call Christian countries and Muslim countries—but as secular countries.

One cryptic conclusion from Karren Armstrong's book is– "religion has been changing in its native form, practice, ideology, conception etc and has been influenced by several other religions/ faiths/cults/views and hence has been changing a lot- hence lot of scope for both genuine and intentional debates"—(**Self**- To what Karren Armstrong said one may add enormous developments in Science and Technology and the availability of a wide variety of goods and services since the inception of the religion till today. And nothing to be surprised if some more changes occur in future times. There are thousands of theses on Shakespeare. When Shakespeare has written his works, he might have meant what he has written in some specific manner but the subsequent researchers/scholars have analysed him and produced thousands of theses. Had Shakespeare been alive probably he would have rejected many theses. He is not here to approve or disapprove what others have written about his works. Similarly so with so many authors and works. So the book can be the same but the understanding of the book can genuinely vary with time, place and persons or what is written in the book is applied keeping in view the contemporary circumstances. This happens/can happen with any religion or philosophy. As long as one does not trouble others it should not matter as to whatever ideology one follows. After all, the ultimate purpose of every one is the same. To live in peace and harmony. Of course the fighting between two people—even two brothers-or two groups of people need not be always because of reasons of God/ practicing of religion/ ideology. There could be other reasons. In different societies the reasons are stated differently. For example, wealth and women; wealth, women and land/territory; power and pelf (wealth). Hindus have identified the strong emotions as reasons Viz; : Anger, lust, greed, infatuation, arrogance/pride and jealousy. Hence Hinduism places strong emphasis on controlling these emotions to prevent fightings/conflicts. One can add in the modern days—scarcity of resources. UNESCO Constitution 1945 /1946 declares–"That since wars begin in the minds of men, it is in the minds of men that the defences of peace must be constructed"; That ignorance of each other's ways and lives has been a common cause, throughout the history of mankind, of that suspicion and mistrust between the peoples of the world through which their differences have all too often broken into war; etc).

I once again swear that I have not become blasphemous to any religion but only tried to cater for the intentions of curious public both ordinary and qualified in the modern era across the globe. Primary aim and hope kept in mind while writing this book and the expectation from the readers across the globe is that "We Should All Live in Peace and Harmony".

I sincerely care for your valuable feedback **<asraobio@gmail.com>**

Chapter - 1

A. Introduction along with Allah's compassionate promises to men

While there can be genuinely more than one way of starting the introduction, I wish to start by first mentioning the structure and organisation of Quraan, followed by five pillars of Islam which I think is one of the important ways of talking about Islam and then mention the other prescriptions (do's and dont's)/some important basic tenets/ basic beliefs in Quraan/Islam. **But I wish to emphasise that one should keep the following highly magnanimous and merciful condonations given by Allah/Prophet to the people--"Allah puts no burden on any person beyond what HE has given him." " Allah does not impose on any soul duties and responsibilities beyond its ability to bear them" (Surah As-Sajdah 32: 53). "Allah desireth your ease. HE desireth not hardship for you. (Surah Al-Baqarah-2:185)" "Allah tasketh not a soul beyond its scope (2:286)". Similar condonations are mentioned in Quraan in several other contexts. What is the essence of these codonations is, one should not wilfully transgress what has been prescribed. And prophet never wanted anyone to be punished with retrospective effect but only if one transgresses after he has prescribed something. So punishment on earth is a very delicate and difficult task as everyone need to be judged thoroughly nor Allah would punish a person ignoring His condonations. These are very important points.**

First, it means that persons have been created by HIM with different capabilities and strengths. Leave aside normal people who also vary a lot in their capabilities and strengths. Besides there are in the world nearly a billion people suffer from so many ailments— Mental disorders/Psychiatric disorders, Congenital abnormalities/ inborn errors of metabolism, spastic people, dementias, and other disabilities like deaf and dumb, etc. Of course the incidence may vary from country to country. Hence these people have genuine inability to varying extents to follow the different prescriptions and need to be condoned accordingly. As to why Allah has created/made them like that ? Only Allah knows. Other religions also say so that only almighty knows the reason.(**Self**-In those religions which believe in rebirth and multiple births some other explanation also is given).

In view of what is mentioned and explained above it is only fair that punishments and /or atonements have to be decided on an individual basis—case by case –approach. And the local custodians in charge of administering punishments and/or atonements have to be highly capable, compassionate, merciful and thoroughly understanding the individuals concerned in all their aspects and keep in mind the above mentioned merciful condonations by Allah/Prophet. So it is a time taking process and punishments and/or atonements may not be administered instantly but only after a thorough understanding of the individuals state of affairs coupled with compassion. Allah knows what is concealed in your hearts.

Secondly, these statements also tells that one will not be punished and it is not to be considered as a sin if one cannot follow what all that is prescribed in case it is genuinely beyond one's capacity and one does not transgress intentionally. In other words it also means that different individuals may not be able to genuinely follow different prescriptions and they are to/will be vindicated. And Prophet also was very kind enough to say-past is past.

The terms Islam, Muslims do figure in Quraan itself. Hence the name of the religion and the name for the followers are already mentioned in the Quraan. So they have come to usage during the life of Prophet itself though people may differ on the exact time.

B. Structure and Organisation of Surahs in Quraan (See also "D", Revelation and Compilation of Quraan)

Most important observation is—The entire Quraan—spanned over nearly 23 years with 6236/6238 verses (Ayats)—is solely a one-sided revelation/speech from Angel Gabriel (Jibreel) to Prophet Muhammad. There is no two-way conversation between

Gabriel and Prophet Muhammad. People may get a doubt as to why Prophet Muhamamd did not clarify anything from Gabriel by asking questions but simply listened to him. No one knows, why? A feeling of people could be, even if Prophet would have asked some doubts, very likely that Gabriel would have been glad to entertain them and make the things more explicit. (Many say including Picthall that there are 6666 verses in Quraan but it does not seem to be so. In none of the three Quraans mentioned above including that of Picthall there are 6666 verses. There are only either 6236 or 6238 verses).

There are 114 Surahs (may be called chapters) in the Quraan and 554 sections. Darussallaam version does not indicate the sections, but only verses (called **Ayats**). Every Surah has the caption of **"Bismillahi-Rahmaanir Rahim"** translated as "In the name of the Allah the (Most) Beneficient, the (Most) Merciful except one (9th Surah). This caption does not form the part of revelation—but apparently because of the compilers-though the attributes mentioned in the caption are mentioned in the Quraan frequently.

The Surahs are highly unequal in length. The Surahs vary a lot in the number of sections and number of verses (Ayats) under a section. Therefore, the number of verses in a Surah varies widely. The length of verses (Ayats) also vary. It can be as short as a single sentence with few words. Salient points are as follows. Number of sections in a Surah vary from 1 to 40 and the number of verses in a Surah may vary from as low as 3 to a maximum of 286. There are 36 Surahs with just one section and the number of verses in this one section can vary from 3 to 42. There are 22 Surahs with just two sections and the verses vary from 12 to 52. Ten Surahs with three sections and verses vary from 30 to 78. Five Surahs with four sections and the verses vary from 29 to 37. Another five Surahs with five sections and the verses vary from 45 to 182. Eight Surahs with six sections and verses vary from 43 to 118. Seven Surahs with five sections and verses vary from 52 to 112. Two Surahs with eight sections and verses are 75 and 135 in each of the Surah. Four Surahs with nine sections and verses vary from 64 to 88. Three Surahs with ten sections with verses 75, 123 and 78. Two Surahs with eleven sections with verses 109 and 227.

Two Surahs with twelve Sections with verses 111 and 110. Three Surahs with sixteen sections with verses 120, 129 and 128. Two Surahs with twenty sections with verses 200 and 166. Two Surahs with twenty four sections with verses 176/177 and 206 verses.

One Surah with forty sections and 286 verses, named Al-Baqarah (The Cow) is the largest Surah and also has the longest verse-number 282-but the number of words (in English translation) in this verse slightly vary in the above mentioned three Quraans; 275 in Picthall, 259 in Darussalam and 256 in Saudi. The point to be noted here is, different bilingual-English-Arabic, literature academicians may translate the verses differently. And some may be capable of making translations both accurately and also with lesser number of words. Of course brevity should not be at the expense of clarity.

In some Surahs many verses are just of a single sentence that too of few words. And such ayats on their own may not reflect any meaning but one may have to read other such single sentence ayats preceding and /or following it in that particular Surah. Difficult to imagine the time span of revelation of such large number of "single sentence Ayats". Unless they are revealed as a whole it would take time to make some meaning out of them.

The proper name of each Surah is prefixed with ar/as/al/az/ad,/ at/an/ash which indicates the English article "The". For Example, Al-Quraan or Al Fatiha meaning The Quraan or The opening.

The number of verses seem to vary in different versions of the Quraan. While in the Medinah (Saudi) Quraan and Darussalaam Quran the number of verses are 6236, in Pickthall they are 6238. (However, Pickthall states in his introduction that 6666 verses are there in Quraan). As the revelations have occurred both during Mecca and Medinah, it is natural to be inquisitive to know as to how many are revealed in these places. This information is again different in different versions of the Quraan. In the Saudi Quraan and Darussalaam Quran 4613 verses (approximately 74 per cent of the total Quraan verses) are revealed in Mecca and 1623 verses (approximately 26 per cent of the total Quraan verses) in Medinah while in Picthall 4807 verses (approximately 77 per cent of the total Quran Verses) were revealed in Mecca and 1431 verses (approximately 23 per cent of the total

Quraan verses). Prophet seemed to have stayed for nearly twelve years in Mecca counting from the first revelation and nearly ten years in Medinah. (But while in Medinah he did visit Mecca twice for different periods of time). So one can imagine the wide difference in the magnitude of revelations in spite of only a slight difference in the duration of his stay in Mecca and Medinah. However, Prophet happened to give many important recommendations from Medinah. In terms of number of Surahs, 93 out of 114 are revealed in Mecca and 21 in Medinah as per Picthall. And as per Saudi and Darussallam Quraans 86 Surahs are revealed in Mecca and 28 in Medinah. So according to Picthall, in terms of number of Surahs, approximately 82 per cent of the total Quraan Surahs (that is 93/114) have been revealed in Mecca and approximately 18 per cent of the total Quraan Surahs (21/114) have been revealed in Medinah. Some of the Medinah surahs are very long. Four Medinah Surahs Viz; number 2, 4, 5 and 10 have number of verses in three digits and contribute to approximately 50 per cent of the total Medinah Surahs.

According to Saudi/Darussalam, in terms of number of Surahs, approximately 75 per cent of the total Quraan Surahs (86/114) have been revealed in Mecca and approximately 25 per cent of the total Quraan Surahs (28/114) have been revealed in Medinah. This is again as mentioned above is because, some of the Medinah surahs are very long. Four Medinah Surahs viz; number 2, 4, 5 and 10 have number of verses in three digits and contribute to approximately 44 per cent of the total Medinah Surahs. Picthall version has seven more Meccan Surahs compared to the other two Quraan versions. However, according to J. M. Rodwell's Quraan, there are 6133 verses. Rodwell differs a lot in the order in which Surahs are arranged. First 90 Surahs are of Meccan -with the exception of two Surahs which have been indicated as doubtful whether they belong to Mecca or Medinah—followed by 23 Medinah Surahs and with one Meccan Surah between. So as per the above calculations in Rodwell's Quraan, 4665 (approximately 76 per cent of the total Quraan verses) are revealed in Mecca and 1457 (approximately 24 per cent of the total Quraan verses) in Medinah. The two doubtful verses together constitute only 11 verses. In terms of Surahs in Rodwell, approximately 78 per cent of the total Quraan Surahs (89/114) have been revealed in Mecca and approximately 20 per cent of the total Quraan Surahs (23/114) have been revealed in Medinah.

(**Self**-- Rodwell differs in so many aspects and I am not concerned with that in the present write up. That is something for scholars of Abrahamic religions).

According to Phillip Hitti, also there are 6236 Verses (as found in the above two mentioned Quraans) and there are 3,23,621 (three lakhs twenty three thousand and six hundred and twenty one letters. So apparently in case the number of verses are different in any version of Quraan, the number of letters also would vary. I am really impressed and appreciate the pains of the person (maybe Phillip Hiitti himself) who has counted the total number of letters. I was motivated by this and I got the idea of counting the number of times "Allah" has been mentioned in the Quraan. I might have been little deficient in my attention and concentration while counting. The number I counted–2712—can be right or more or even less. (This number excludes the mentioning of "Allah" within brackets by the authors at so many places. Further words like "Lord", "HE", "HIM" also are used referring to Allah and such words are not taken into counting by me. If they are also included in the counting the number can be still high.). May all of you and Allah forgive me if the number quoted is less. However, I am happy that I have counted a higher number -2712- compared to two other sites on Google—http://orbitislam.com/100-questions-on-quran/which gives a total figure of 2698. Another site on Google gives a number of 2584. However, these sites have not mentioned further details about their manner of counting as I mentioned above. There can be some more sites where this number is quoted and information regarding this aspect may vary.

(If my concentration is right, there is no mention of Allah in the Surahs viz; 54, 55, 68, 75,77, 78, 86, 89, 90, 93, 94, 99 to 103, 107 to 109, 111, 113, and 114 i.e. at least in 22 Surahs there is no mention of Allah and in 15 Surahs Allah's name is mentioned only once. The maximum number of times (280) the name is mentioned in Surah 2, followed by Surah 4 (223), Surah 3 (213),.Surah 9 (161), Surah 5 (149) and 33 (107).

Prescriptions/verses related to the same issue/topic are covered under different Surahs and even in the same Surah more than one topic/issue has been discussed. Sometimes prescriptions may fall both under Meccan and Medinah Surahs. Hence the captions given to the Surahs are not pertaining to the entire number of verses in the Surah. How captions for all 114 Surahs have been selected is not clear for all Surahs. Titles of Surahs are not by Gabriel but by compilers. All Ayats under a surah may not justify the caption of a Surah, even in cases where the caption pertains to a specific issue/topic. What I said above is also clear from the elaborate index and Introduction and Summary of every Surah mentioned in medinah (Saudi) Quraan. Further some Surahs are titled with the mysterious abbreviated letters (Al-Muqattaat) whose meaning is believed to be known only to Allah (discussed below). So it is all the more surprise as to how the compilers have selected these as the title of some Surahs.

C. Repetitions in Quraan

There are so many points and expressions which are repeated several times in the Quraan-either as such or with a slight change but essence/meaning remaining the same. Apparently considerable space is devoted to these repetitions. One definitely may wonder as to how so much redundancy is there? Did Angel Gabriel repeated so many times the same thing?? Or this redundancy has crept because of the way it has been compiled? It is up to the Abrahamic scholars to take up the exercise. However, I feel, to facilitate an easy and fast learning of Quraan, for any one, Muslims, non-Muslims (both Abrahamic and non-Abrahamic religions (developed or folk), Atheists/ Agnostics etc (collectively referred to as "Unaffiliated" in world census) the size of the Quraan probably can be reduced if repetitions are deleted wherever possible. **The essence is not going to change. Such a publication also will be a grand sale.**

Here, I am mentioning many points, if not all—what has been frequently repeated in the Quraan either *in toto* or with a slight change in the words retaining the same meaning. One may probably infer that such repeated points reflect that they are very important for the devotees to keep in mind. Or as Medinah Quraan states the Quraan was revealed in stages as per the demand of the occasion. So maybe the occasions to repeat the points arose so many times. But these inferences may not be convincing. And people are very likely to attribute them to compilers of the Quraan. Broadly the repetitions belong to the attributes of Allah, prescriptions to follow—do's and dont's-, some expressions whose meaning is known only to Allah and some other basic beliefs:

Examples of Repetitions-

(a)

1. Unto Allah belongs whatever is in the heavens and whatever in the earth/Allah created heaven and earth and all in between them. 2. Allah is forgiving and merciful. (In one version of the Quraan the same translation is made as "Allah is Oft-forgiving and merciful". This can be understood differently. When the word "Oft" is used it may convey the meaning that in general Allah is forgiving and merciful but Allah always does not forgive and is not always merciful. So when HE is not so, it is not clear,). 3. Allah loveth not aggressors. 4. Allah Loveth the Beneficent. 5. Allah is strong/ severe in punishment. 6. Allah is mighty and wise. 7. Allah is all embracing and all knowing. 7. Allah is (ever) knower of all things. 8. Allah is (ever) witness of all things. 9. Allah is hearer and knower. 10. Allah is knower and wise. 11. Allah is ever exalted, high and great. 12. Allah loveth not proud and boastful. 13. Allah is ever hearer and seer. 14. Allah is all embracing and all knowing. 15. Allah loveth the good. 16. Allah is with the steadfast. 17. Praise be to Allah. 18. There is no God save Him. 19. He is the protector. 20. Signs of Allah particularly with reference to last day of judgement. 21. Rejecting the signs of Allah. 22. One who send rain from the sky. 23. These are the verses of the book. 24. Allah is witness to all things. 25. Creation in six days. 26. Allah knows what is concealed in your heart.

(b)

In addition to the above 1 to 26, the following words, affirmations and diktats are **repeated several times** in Quraan; for example—believers; non-believers/infidels; idolaters; Prayers; Zakat; last day of judgement and signs of last day of judgement; alms and charity; chastisement; biblical characters and narrations; pagans; Lo! (This single word expression was used so many times in the Quraan of Picthall but its usage is negligible if at all in the other two Quraans. It definitely needs to be clarified whether in the original Arabic Ayats whether there is any corresponding Arabic word. If it is not there then Picthall has taken too much freedom in using the above expression. If it is there then the other two Quraans have neglected translating the corresponding Arabic word in the Ayats); follow what all Allah has forbidden; you have been created from (a drop of) sperm (**Self**-but it is important to remember that according to Bible and which is also apparently acknowledged by Islam, the very first man Adam was not created from sperm/fluid but from dust and breath into the nostrils by the Lord and the man became a living soul. So it is evident that the soul is divine. Even the second person "Eve" was not created from sperm but from the rib of the Adam and there is no mention as to whether God breathed into the nostrils of Eve or not. We should presume so. Apparently people created afterwards also have the souls which are divine (ensoulment) and what can be created from a drop of sperm can only be a body.(**Self-** However as everything on this earth and elsewhere has been created by God—and no one else has created them—therefore they are all entitled to be referred to as Divine. All things created in the Genesis chapter (old testament) and all those existing before creations like Angels etc are by God only. Not only soul. So it should not be blasphemous to say that everything is of divine origin or divine. Because, who else has created it ? Can you question further ? Who created God ? You can. But you should agree to the answer that God is always present all by himself. No one has created HIM. As the Bible says "neither he is begotten nor he begets". The same thing is said in Quraan too-Lam yalid, wa lam yuulaad **(112: 3).**

Other expressions repeated are : Created you from dust/clay; last day of judgement/day of resurrection; worship Allah and no other God; from earth you came and return back to earth (Bible states "From the dust I created thee and unto the dust I return thee"); raising from the dead, Praise no God but Allah; obey/worship/fear Allah; Allah and his messenger; believers are those who believe in Allah and his messenger;

(d)

Further repetitions include: obey Allah and his messenger (This statement is probably ambiguous. Who said so ? Apparently Gabriel. Was he referring to Prophet Muhammad always? Though Gabriel addressed Prophet in other contexts, but in this context no where it is clearly stated as Prophet Muhammad or said “obey Allah and last messenger”. Whether Gabriel told that Prophet Muhammad is the last messenger is not clear from the English translations. Only at one place it appears that, maybe according to Arabic language/interpretation, Prophet Muhammad is declared as the last messenger i.e. **Surah Ahzaab (The clans/The Confederates, 33: 40**: which states that “Muhammad is not the father of any man among you but he is the messenger of Allah and the Seal of the Prophets”. The word “Seal” is apparently being inferred as indicating the “last”. However, the English translation is not beyond doubt. Seal may simply mean that he is recognised as a prophet. Even if we take some Islamic authors view that it is this verse that indicates Prophet Muhammad as the last messenger, even then, this is the only verse where it means so. In no other verse it is so mentioned. However, the simpler expression “Allah and His messenger is repeated many times. As to when Gabriel has told **33:40** is also not clear except for that, this Surah is of Medinah i.e. at least after 10 yrs of prophet hood or more.);

(e)

Some more repetitions in Quraan include: there is no God but He; give what is due to the kindred, the needy and the wayfarer; be good to parents (mother and father); in the end you return to me; paganism/idolatry should be abolished; sends rain/and producing grain; those who reject Allah/book/signs-fire of hell; revelation of the book is from Allah; rejecting the signs of Allah; serve none but Allah; day/night/sky/heaven/earth made by Allah; children of Israel; biblical characters (both of old and new testament); (Gabriel often uses the addressing “We” for example by saying “we have”, “we made”, “we took”, “we gave/we did give”, “we said”, “We who revealed” etc. Whom all Gabriel is referring by saying “We” is not clear. One has to only speculate. This exercise is again for the Abrahamic scholars); HE forgives whom he will and punishes whom HE wills; God created heaven and earth in six days (but Prophet has changed the day of Sabbath being followed by Jews); Allah puts no burden on any person beyond what He has given him (many Ayats with similar meaning are mentioned at different places. **Most important have been mentioned above in Bold Sentences**; care/feed the poor, orphans (do not exploit the orphans in any way) ; neighbours and the captives; ask forgiveness; mention of some of the forbidden things ; for example, eating of swine flesh, usury, adultery, etc, (**The above mentioned in different paragraphs-a-e and f mentioned below—are the most common repetitions**). One can easily find some more.

Though there are 114 Surahs and 6236/ 6238 verses, Gabriel rarely seemed to have addressed individually/directly, as Muhammad. Even addressing directly as Prophet i.e. as Oh ! Prophet, Gabriel did so only six times, four times in the Surah 33, Ahzaab (The clans/The Confederates) and once in each of the two Surahs, 65 and 66. However, by saying Oh! Muhammad! Gabriel has not addressed even once, though Muhammad's name is mentioned four times and one Surah is named after Muhammad (But the naming of Surahs is not by Gabriel but by the compilers. Further the verses in this surah are similar to verses in other Surahs and do not specifically mention 'Muhammad' anymore.). Islamic authors consider the mention of Ahmad as an equivalent of Muhammad's and even Ahmad is mentioned only once.

(f)

Significance/Mystery of Abbreviated letters(Al—Muqattat). Some are repeated and some are not. There are many words in Quraan which are given at the beginning of the Surah—not in the beginning of all Surahs but in many Surahs-but whose meaning is not there but is simply stated that the meaning of these words are known only to Allah or some other meaning in some cases. In some cases these words are counted in the number of verses and in some does not seem to be counted as verses. Medinah (Saudi) Quraan gives a good picture about these letters.

In all there are only 29 Surahs with abbreviated letters (given as English letters). These letters are found either as single letters or as a combination of letters:

A.L. M. (Surah 2 and 3); Alif, Laam, Miim, Saad (Surah 7); A.L.R (Surahs 10,11, 12, 14, 15); A.L.M.R (Surah 13); A.L.M.(Surahs 29, 30, 31, 32); Haa miim (40, 41, 42, 43, 44, 45, 46); Taa siim Miim (Surahs 26 and 28); Kaaf Haa yaa ain Sad (Surah 19); Taa siin (Surah 27); Saad (Surah 38); Yaa siin (Surah 36); Ain Siin Qaaf (Surah 42—this is in addition to Haa Miin in the same Surah); Qaaf (Surah 50).

These abbreviated letters are at the first ayat of the Surahs except in case of Surah 42 where even the second ayat is of abbreviated letters. In some surahs the abbreviated letters are mentioned totally as independent but in some surahs Viz; 10, 11, 12, 13, 14, 15, 27, 38, and 50 are followed by some other words. Interestingly in some Surahs the abbreviated letters are put as the title of the Surahs and also further followed by the same letters as the first ayat in the Surah Viz; Surah 50 (Qaaf), Surah 20 (Ta haa) and Surah 36 (Yaa Siin). Why the compilers of Quraan have put these abbreviated letters—whose meaning is not known–as the title of some Surahs is not clear. Further the title of the Surah "Sad" is followed by three other words appear in the Surah 19:1. In appendix 1 Medina (Saudi) Quraan states that " A number of conjectures have been made to their meaning and opinions are divided as to the exact meaning of each particular letter or combination of letters and finally says **"it is agreed that only Allah knows their exact meaning. In fact the other Quraans also state that only Allah knows their meaning".**

As the Medina Quraan states that "A number of conjectures have been made to their meaning and opinions are divided as to the exact meaning of each particular letter or combination of letters, in other words it means that there is a freedom and that it is permitted to interpret these letters and combination of letters by at least clergy/scholars. Naturally these interpretations may vary and with time in future many meanings may come. It is not clear whether it is permissible to give the meanings of these letters in Quraan, as on today it is said that 'Only Allah knows their exact meaning.' " Maybe the respective clergy will take a decision on this. It is also not clear as to how it has been decided to count the mentioning of these letters towards the total number of Ayats and has to be put in the beginning of the Ayat of a particular Surah. Further it may also mean that the meaning of these words was not revealed even to prophet and even prophet did not ask Gabriel to reveal the meaning.

(**Self-**it is stated **repeatedly** in Quraan that the **meaning** of the above words is **known only to Allah.** In other words it can mean that one can never know the meaning of the above words even till Qiyamat. If that is so why they have been revealed ? What is their utility ? Is it possible that Allah sends someone before Qiyamat at some time in future and reveal the meaning of the above words ! ? As mentioned above as per Medinah Quraan some conjectures have been made and so many may do so in future too. But we cannot speculate as to when, whose and what meaning will be unanimously accepted, if at all it happens.

In addition to the above it appears there are some more or may be considerable even whose meaning is known only to Allah. Ayat **3.7** states that Allah has made some revelations very clearly while some revelations in an allegoric manner or in a manner whose meaning only Allah knows. So we should apparently function on the basis of those revelations which are made in a clear manner. But how to know which are the revelations which have been revealed in a clear manner? Who is to tell us? Out of the 6236/6238 Ayats how many are clearly revealed and how many are not? On the basis of **3.7** ayat this is a very important piece of information and only scholars can do this. And whenever such an exercise is taken it quite likely that there can be genuine differences. And they need to be resolved. **If a Quraan version is published after doing the above exercise that would be another grand commercial venture /sale of the book.**

(**Self**—In view of the above, it would be an **useful reorganisation of Quraan--**not to replace the existing ones—but as a valuable addition if a Quraan is compiled : (a) pooling up all the relevant verses belonging to a specific prescription/topic from different Surahs (b) removing or minimising as much as possible the repetitions mentioned above, (c) making a clear cut demarcations between prescriptions given by Gabriel in Mecca and in Medinah i.e. prescriptions exclusively made in Mecca and prescriptions made exclusively in Medinah. Some idea of the some basic tenets is evident from a study of the chronology of prophet. What is Medinah period must be clearly demarcated. Because after Hijra, Prophet did visit Mecca twice and stayed there for different times. So revelations during that time will have to be classified as Meccan only, though Prophet was staying at Medinah during that period. Obviously it requires the arrangement of all Meccan Surahs in the beginning from 610 to 622 followed by all Medinah Surahs from 622 to 632/633 with the exception of any revelations of Surahs during Prophet's visits to Mecca. Of course this will not tell the exact time sequence of the revelations of the various Surahs/verses in that particular place. The Saudi Quraan classifies Surahs as early Meccan, late Meccan etc. In case they are arranged in that sequence some idea of time sequence of revelations will be known if not in entirety. If prescriptions are repeated both in Mecca and Medinah then naturally they should be included under Mecca and avoided in Medinah. A Quraan with such an arrangement will be shorter and easier to learn. (d) making a clear cut demarcation of what is accepted of the past in the Abrahamic religions and of other prophets acknowledged specifically by Islam and what is not accepted of them and what is new to be practiced as revealed to Prophet Muhammad. My above recommendation is justified in view of the information given in Medina (Saudi) version of Quraan. Some information has been mentioned above. Further, in justification it may be said that ayat **10:17** states that Quraan is a confirmation of (revelations) that went before it and a fuller explanation of them. It is not clear what all points have been explained in detail and how that details of those points were, initially? More importantly in Appendix 3 of medinah Quraan it is stated that "Quraan does not *in toto* refer/accept to the Bible *in toto* but only to fragments of New and old testament and only these have to be accepted. Views other than these of either Jews or Christians are not accepted by Islam. So it should be made clear by the Scholars/clergy as to what fragments of Bible are accepted and what are not. Apparently not much of Bible is accepted (however so many surahs and descriptions of biblical characters are mentioned in Quraan which makes the task difficult. Further Bible is divided into Old and New Testaments and relevant to two more religions, Christianity and Judaism. Judaism of course does not give importance to New Testament).

So Islam saying that they accept or do not accept Bible (Old and New Testaments)–both statements are right.

In view of the above a Quraan which is reorganised taking into consideration all of the above is a welcome move. Rather there is a scope for compiling more than one book.

According to many from Adam to Prophet Muhammad, there were 1,24,000 prophets. A very large number. Neither we have a complete list of them nor of what they have taught. And it is also not clear, whether the above number of prophets were all counted from Abrahamic religions or does it include from other religions too ? ? Quraan does not state the above details. Ayat **3:144** simply states that many messengers have passed away before Prophet Muhammad).

(D) Revelation and Compilation of Quraan (see the above mentioned "B", Structure and Organisation of Quraan)

Quraan-The term meaning "Recitation" as Gabriel asked the Prophet Muhammad to recite what all he said. It is a revelation of Allah through the Angel Gabriel. It is not a revelation at a single stretch, but spread over at least 22-23 years (23 more quoted) apparently with some time gaps in between and revealed at different places. At one place-rather at only one place- the above observation is in fact mentioned in Quraan—Surah, Al-Isra/Binii israaiil- **17: 106**. Strangely the Surah in which such a statement is made about revelation of Quraan is named as Al-Isra/Binii israaiil i.e. "The children of Israel"! Maybe in those days people, not only in the present day Israel but people in regions around also were being referred to as, Children of Israel. The above verse (ayat) in the Surah states "A Quraan, which we have divided in order that thou might recite it to men at intervals; we have revealed it by stage. It appears a different explanation is given in the Ayat **25: 32.** Here it is said that the Quraan was not revealed at a stretch because revealing at intervals will strengthen the heart (either of the Prophet and /or others). However, an important doubt may arise in the minds of the people. Suppose the entire Quraan is revealed at a stretch will it be possible for the Prophet to remember all the 6326/6328 ayats ? Is it possible for him to remember and /or make arrangements to note all of them? By the Grace of Allah it is possible. For Moses it is believed to habe revealed at a stretch. (**Self-** However, what exactly Gabriel revealed; which verses at which time and for what situation/ purpose meant for that time is not known.

This is really an important information missing. We do not know whether any archives will be available now to throw some light on this. It was an exercise that should have been done during the time of Prophet or soon after the death of the Prophet when Quraan was being compiled taking the help of those who have noted down the recitations from the prophet and /or those who have supposed to have memorised the entire Quraan-called Huffaz/Hafiz. One may differ as to how many such people were there? According to one site, there were 22 Huffaz-memorizers who were associates of prophet and Abu Bakar took the help of 75 people at the time of compiling the Quraan. Subsequently, both the people and the number might have changed, as and when another Quraan got compiled.). Medinah Quraan says an additional point. Quraan has been revealed in stages as and when there is a demanding occasion.

The language of Quraan is Arabic—to be more specific Qureshi dialect of Arabic. At that time there were some other dialects too. Now dialects have become nearly extinct. And the Quraan is translated into Modern Standard Arabic (MSA), though the original Qureshi dialect revelation is maintained as sacred. Quran is praised for its inimitable beauty of the language. So the question comes to what extent Modern Standard Arabic comes close to the original Quraan revealed in the Qureshi dialect!?

The possibility of others raising doubts about revelation was raised by Gabriel himself

11 :13- "if someone says Quraan is not a revelation but invented, tell to them to compose and bring ten surahs of the standard available in Quraan". (**Self-**As Muhammad was not literate no one can say that he has invented the Surahs/Ayats. So we do not know why Gabriel said so. Obviously the invention if at all has to be from some others and not Muhammad. Were there any great scholars available in Qureshi dialect at that time who used to compose high standard literature? Now the dialect might have/apparently has become extinct and is replaced by modern standard Arabic).

(**Self-** Gabriel definitely must be knowing the languages spoken by Jesus, Moses, Abraham etc. Hebrew and Aramaic. But these languages were not used for revelation to Prophet. Apparently this is because the person chosen for revelation -Prophet Muhammad—was knowing only the Qureshi dialect of Arabic. "As on today according to Karren Armstrong, different dialects of Arabic are not there and Arabs seem to speak what is called as modern standard Arabic (MSA)..And Quraan has been rewritten in modern standard Arabic as well and translated into several other languages.". But since revelation was in Qureshi dialect and the Quraan is read as such as well this dialect is apparently alive only to this extent. **(Self-Authors/compilers of Medinah Quraan (used synonymously as Saudi Quraan) say that revelation come to each nation in its own language and for its own special circumstances.** A corollary of this is, Quran is apparently is entirely valid only for the nation/place where it was revealed—Mecca and Medinah in Saudi Arabia—and the circumstances then prevailing in this nation/place. For other nations/ places in the globe—in any case outside the Arab belt the Quraan is not probably entirely valid as circumstances in these nations were different. More so in the present times—nearly1400 years after Quraan was revealed—when state of affairs in the society have drastically changed, even in the Arab belt. Further Ayat **14:4** says that "We sent not a messenger except (to teach) in the language of his (own) people in order to make (things) clear to them". So now the question is whom the Gabriel is referring to? Only messengers of the Abrahamic religions? If so it is probably mainly two languages earlier—Hebrew and Aramaic which were later translated. What is said also means that there has to be as many messengers as there are languages on the globe. Then only things will be clear and reliable for everyone. Further for reason mentioned above by the Saudi authors—preachings are based on the circumstances prevailing in the particular nations. Hence many preachings—what to follow and what not to follow—are very likely to be different from nation to nation and even in the same nation from time to time in view of the varying circumstances. Hence additional prophets/messengers are required intermittently with changing circumstances in future too).

Translation is presently available apparently in about 100 languages including "modern standard Arabic". It is not known how many read the original Qureshi dialect and how many read in "modern standard Arabic" and how many read in their respective languages.

Of course, prayer is mandatory to be in original Arabic. Translations are quite natural to happen and it is so with Bible too. I think in view of so many languages around the world others also should resort to translations of the original texts in all religions and faiths and ideologies in their respective native languages. This will definitely help people to understand and interact better. Further Gabriel has chosen the word "Allah" which was not used either in Old Testament or in New Testament. In Bible words like God, Lord, Lord God, Holy Father, Yehowa etc. were used. This is apparently because Quraan was revealed in Arabic and "Allah" is an Arabic word whose equivalents have to be the above mentioned words and in addition—Almighty, Supreme, Super Power, in English and similarly we have equivalent words in various languages of the world. Of course in Quraan though Allah is primarily used, the terms "Lord", God also are used in English translations. Why in some places the terms "Lord" or "God" is used instead of Allah is not clear?

In view of the above–that is, as there is no mention of the word "Allah" in the Bible Old or New Testament the Ayats **"61.5** and **61.6 and 5 :114** will not be accepted ***in toto*** by the Christians and probably even by Jews. In the above Ayats it is said that Moses and Jesus have told that they are messengers of "Allah". So very likely one of the above mentioned words or some Aramaic or Hebrew word might have been used by Moses and Jesus and it was translated as "Allah" in the Arabic Quraan.

Islam does not consider Jesus, angels or spirits, or other prophets on par with the Almighty/Supreme. Quite justified. In fact, it is so with other religions too. The differences in others is a different story (See general remarks at the end). Almighty or Supreme cannot be two ! It is definitely one and only one. There is nothing like "my God", "your God ", "our God", "their God" etc. It does not make sense. There is only one God and HE is the same for all. Not only me, so many believe so and the differences with others is a different story).

(**Self-**Gabriel/Quraan has devoted considerable space in Quraan for biblical characters and narrations! How much of it is because of Gabriel's revelation and how much is because of compilation/ compilers we do not know. But considerable space is allotted to biblical characters and narrations. Six Surahs have been named after them Viz; Surahs: 3-(Ali Imran-The Family of Imran (Amram); 10-(Yunus-Jonah); 12-(Yusuf- Joseph); 14-(Ibrahim-Abraham); 19-(Maryam-Mary); 71-(Nuh-Noaha) apart from repeating biblical characters and narrations in other surahs. Why Gabriel has to repeat so much of the past history and past prophets and religions when he was preaching afresh to a new Prophet is something that people may think? Is it because prophet was not aware of the past? Little bit of mention can be more easily understood. Did Gabriel narrated everything as mentioned in the bible? (**See remarks of Medinah (Saudi) Quraan mentioned above**). Had Gabriel's revelation be compiled in such a manner indicating what of the past is to be followed or not to be followed and what afresh he expects to follow, that would have made the revelation more clear and less debatable. Even if Gabriel has mentioned a lot, why the compilers preferred to name six Surahs in the name of prophets of the past two religions with whom they have fallen apart as a separate identity? The manner of biblical narrations also gives an impression that Quraan/Islam tries to interpret all the biblical characters and narrations in their favour. Leave aside others, will even the other two Abrahamic religions, Judaism and Christianity agree to this? The issue is best left to the scholars and religious custodians of the other two religions. However, some eminent and authoritative academicians can educate the rest of the world. Someone or collectively should write a book comparing and contrasting the three Abrahamic religions, point wise. In other words, is Gabriel's revelation-Quraan-to be treated as in addition to what has been already told earlier to other prophets (at least of other Abrahamic religions) or it makes what has earlier been told, totally or partially (if so which aspects) null and void? Or what is told to Prophet Muhammad by Gabriel's is a mixture of something already told earlier and something in addition? If it is a mixture how much and what is from the earlier knowledge of the prophets and what has been further added and what has been deleted from what has been already taught to/by the earlier prophets has to be very clearly expressed. This is better done by scholars/clergy from Abrahamic religions working together. **Some views of Medinah (Saudi) Quraan in this regard have been mentioned above**. This exercise is very essential as Islam believes, whether it is a mixture as mentioned above or it is altogether afresh, every other scripture becomes null and void after Quran has come into force. This venture is again going to be a big **commercial venture** apart from spreading knowledge of both regional and universal applicability).

In 610, when Muhammad was 40 he got the revelation on 17th day of Ramadaan. While this statement is widely accepted, there are slight differences of opinion because Prophet himself seem to have said that he had been listening voices much before 40 and only at 40 he got fully convinced about the revelations by Gabriel. Secondly, literature mentions that Prophet got his first revelation in the month of Ramadan on one of the odd days. Hence it need not be 17th only. Could be on any one of the other odd days. Thirdly, while the revelation period everyone has fixed as 610 some are differing in his date of birth; 570 or 569 or 567 ? But 570 is widely accepted and similarly his death date 632 as the date of death is the year quoted in the references given. During the initial period of receiving revelations Prophet Muhammad was supposed to have been overtaken by fear, nervousness and doubt. Subsequently he got convinced and only after sometime after 40-(maybe few years according to Karren Armstrong) he started preaching Quraan. As mentioned above, probably unlike other Prophets, say for example, Moses who was supposed to have got the entire revelation in a single encounter, Prophet Muhammad was getting revelations almost till his death from around 40 yrs i.e. for nearly 23 yrs in varying number of verses, cumulatively all together form the Quraan which was compiled much later after the death of Prophet Muhammad. Now many questions arise. (a) Muhammad, as agreed upon by all could only listen and recite. So what all he has been listening, he obviously might have recited to some others and asked them to note down. To whom all he has told to do so and which portions—over the entire span of 23 yrs— is not known. It is also not known in what manner all of them have noted down and when they have noted down. (b) While it is unanimously agreed that the first revelation was in the month of Ramadaan, difficult to infer anything about all the other revelations. Was every revelation till the death of prophet-spanning nearly 23 yrs—occurred during the month of only Ramadaan i.e. 23 Ramadaans?? Many feel that it was possible to note down at the time of Prophet the exact year, month, date, day and time but unfortunately it has not been done so for the revelations or unfortunately that information is lost. However, a little bit of information is available. Otherwise how could some authors say that there was a time gap of two years and six months between the first and second revelation ? If this is correct then Prophet Muhammad has very little to preach during the above time and probably he had received not just five verses as claimed above but much more. Otherwise Prophet Muhammad has only five verses to preach during the above period.! (c) How many times did Gabriel visit Prophet Muhammad in his entire life? (d) As the length of Surahs and the number of verses in a Surah are highly variable, naturally it means that Gabriel in his visits has apparently taught to different extent. (Surah Al-Isra/Binii israaiil- **17: 106**.) Did Gabriel made a visit, just to teach as low as three verses? (d) Even during Prophet Muhammad's time it was possible to note the year, date, day and even time as per the then existing system (at least broadly as morning, noon, evening, night etc). But it is not known whether Prophet has made arrangements to make any such record as and when he listened to Gabriel or the people to whom he has in turn recited has made any such record? Unfortunately that information either was not there or was lost. Hence we do not know the exact chronological order of the revelations, except for saying that the revelation was made in Mecca or Medina. Some Surahs are controversial whether they were revealed in Mecca or Medinah. Medinah (Saudi) version of the Quraan broadly mentions as early Meccan, late Meccan or early Medinah or late Medinah etc. But even this does not mention the above particulars. We really are missing a very important aspect of revelations in view of the absence of the above particulars. The sequence in which we read the Surahs in the standard Quraans is apparently not the sequence in which Muhammad got the revelation from Gabriel. In none of the three Quraans mentioned, the above information is there, though some people believe that it is possible to arrange the Quraan in a chronological order. But even these people have not confirmed that it is possible to know the date, day and time. Probably what they meant at the most was, only the year in which the revelation occurred could be ascertained. Even without the above particulars if it is possible to arrange the Quraan in chronological order, I feel it should be done and I am sure it will be a **great sale of that compilation** all over the world. (**Self- Other ways of reorganising the Quraan I have mentioned above. In addition another compilation which will turn out to be a grand commercial venture is to organise and sell the books as follows. Muslims believe in what is called as "Fard" which is something backed by Quraan and thus obligatory and "Wajeeb" which is something a Muslim should do but not supported by Quraan but rather ordered by prophet. Apparently Muslims are following what prophet has said (Wajeeb) purely out of reverence to him and tradition. These prescriptions apparently may or may not be judged by Allah at the time of Qiyamat for punishment. So if a scholar can separate clearly these two aspects and publish the books separately it would be a great commercial venture and would also be highly useful for all including non-Muslims.**). (There are some people who are using the words "Fard" and "wajeeb" as synonymous meaning as mandatory and using some other word for what is recommendatory (mandub or mustahabb), but what is mentioned above is accepted widely).

The time when Prophet Muhammad got the revelation and the time when he has preached that revelation to the public may be different. So if this information can be made available then a Quraan published in that order also is of great significance. Presently experts seem to acknowledge the view that what we now have is a random compilation procured from different people and sources after the death of Prophet Muhammad. However, Rodwell differs a lot in arranging the various Surahs in contrast to the standard versions of the Quraans. First, he lists out 90 Meccan Surahs-with two Surahs among them being said as doubtful, followed by 24 Medinah Surahs with the exception of one Meccan Surah among them. An important point to be noted here is, even in the list of Meccan Surahs and Medinah Surahs the order of surahs is different in Rodwell in striking contrast to other standard Quraans. (**Self-**Rodwell differs in so many aspects and I am not concerned with that in the present write up. That is upto scholars of Abrahamic religions).

However, a little bit of definite information seems to be available, in spite of which the organisation of Quraan was not accordingly done!? Why so, it is not clear?

Not clear/convincing? It is agreed that the first five verses of Surah **96-Iqraa/Al-Alaq** were the first direct revelation to the Prophet Muhammad. That is, it should have been around 610 when Prophet Muhammad was forty. Then why these verses are not put in the beginning of the Quraan? In all the Surah has 19 verses. So by inference the other fifteen verses were revealed later. Why the first revealed verses were merged with the later revealed verses? Since they are the first revelation it is worth knowing the meaning of these five verses. They mean "proclaim in the name of the Lord who is the cherisher, most bountiful, who taught the pen and who created you from a leech like clot". (**Self-** Leech like clot refers to an initial stage of human embryonic development in the female uterus. Other than this expression the woman's contribution of "egg" as per the modern science is not mentioned though "sperm drop" is often mentioned). In this first revelation of five verses Gabriel has not used the term "Allah". However, the English translation uses the word 'Lord'. In case Gabriel would have specifically used the word "Allah" as in so many other places, such an English translation cannot come. Even in the remaining 14 verses the word "Allah" comes only once and this Surah has only one section. Such merging of verses as above might have occurred for many other Surahs. According to Saudi Quraan, **the second surah to be revealed** is Al-Qalam -The Pen - 68th surah. (However, like in 73rd surah, here it is not made clear whether the entire Surah is revealed as a whole or in part). The **third surah to be revealed** is 73-Al-Muzzammil (The enshrouded one/Folded in garments. Muzzamil is one of the titles of the prophet.). Even the 74th Surah, Al-Muddaththir (The cloaked ones) is also supposed to be around the same time as that of 68th and 73rd. So these three Surahs should have been placed much earlier in the Quraan. Now they are found in the later parts as clearly revealed by their numbers. Similarly Surah 76-Ad-Dahr/Al-Insaan-Man—is supposed to be of early Meccan period and it is further stated that not all verses in this surah are of early Meccan period. So some verses (Ayats) from a different time were merged. To what extent these periods of time vary we do not know. And we do not know in how many other surahs such a thing—that is merging of verses belonging to different periods of time—has occurred. From the present Quraan organisation it appears that many early Meccan Surahs have been placed in the later parts of the Quraan. Saudi Quraan also states that the following words in the Ayat **5:3** (Al-Maida (The Table spread) "This day have I perfected your religion. For you, completed my favour upon you and have chosen for you Islam as your religion" are the **last words of the Quraan to be revealed**. So it is only natural that one should expect these words at the end of the Quraan but are found in the very early part. Further it is also surprising that these last words are merged with so many other words with some day-to-day prescriptions and these prescriptions have been repeated elsewhere too. So the other words are very likely revealed at some other point of time and have been merged with the last words of the Quraan.

It is also said that the last words of Gabriel are supposed to be from **Surah Ahzaab (The clans/ The Confederates, 33 :40**: which is interpreted as "Muhammad is the last messenger". (further explanation regarding this verse is mentioned elsewhere in the text.). The translation of the entire verse is given above. Hence it should be made very clear unanimously as to what are the last words of the Gabriel? **5 :3** or **33 :40**? And this verse has been apparently been revealed little before Prophets death in 632/633 AD and the surah is considered as a Medinah surah. However, this Surah has in total 73 verses i.e. 72 in addition to the above verse. So why the last words are merged with the rest of the verses? (**Self-**Saudi version of Quraan in this context is little confusing. It states that Surah 110- An-Nasr (Succour /Help) is the last Surah to be revealed as a whole probably a few months before the passing away of Prophet Muhammad. And it is not sure that this Surah is of Meccan or of Medinah. (**Self-** this doubt about the place of Surah is probably because Prophet made a farewell pilgrimage to Mecca before his death and returned to Medinah). This Surah has only three verses and does not have the last words of Gabriel as mentioned above. The Surah Al-Fatiha(The opening) with seven verses is also supposed to have been revealed as a whole.

3:123—Gabriel says—Allah has helped you in the battle of Badr, when you were helpless. (**Self**-The sentence is in past tense and is stating something which has already occurred. So this verse (Ayat) is definitely after the battle of Badr i.e. 13 March 624 when prophet's stay was in Medinah. But this verse is coming in the third chapter (Surah) of the Quraan. A very important observation is, Qibla, Zakat and Fasting, all have been recommended by prophet 14 years after attaining prophethood while Hajj was recommended 21 years after attaining prophet hood. So the years are 624 and 631. (See discussion under Five Pillars of Islam, Chapter II). Because the above are repeated in so many Surahs, the question arises as for the first time when they were mentioned/revealed? As to why Prophet took so much time to recommend the above? Mawlid or Milad Un nabi, is the observance of the birthday of the Islamic Prophet Muhammad which is celebrated in 12 (Sunni)/17 (Shia) Rabi' al-awwal, the third month in the Islamic calendar. It can fall either in November or December. At least to that extent the people to whom Muhammad has told the revelation should have noted it down. As it stands now it is quite likely a random compilation for more than one reason.). (Self—Not only in case of Badr, Gabriel said similarly in **3:144** with reference to battle of Uhud. So Gabriel apparently did not tell priorly about the battles but commented on them after the battles are over).

(**Self**- Another type of analysis can be made. If Quraan is taken as revealed in a span of 23 years (but it is not so, as mentioned above that there is a gap of two and half years between two particular revelations. Even then let us take as 23 years for this analysis. One can alter it if one wants) then it means that 6236 /6238 verses (ayats) are revealed in a span of 23 years. In other words it means approximately 271 verses (Ayats) per year. If we suppose that every time Angel Gabriel revealed Quraan only in the month of Ramadaan, then it means approximately 271 verses per Ramadaan. Now Ramadaan may be 29 days or 30 days. In either case-rounding off the figure-it comes to approximately nine verses (ayats) per day during Ramadaan. (All these figures are inclusive of repetitions mentioned above). If one has a different opinion about the figures mentioned above accordingly one can calculate. All these type of analysis—both in this paragraph and that discussed above—is–at least for the present—purely an academic exercise and what exactly is the sequence of the 6236/6238 verses during the span of 23 years, probably we may never know.

Chapter - 2

Five Pillars of Islam

Islam speaks of Five Pillars of Islam i.e. the five major mandates. **However, all these have not been prescribed at the same time by the Prophet Muhammad or without allowing some exemptions.** We do not know whether time of recommendations of these mandates coincides with the time of Gabriel's revelation of the same to Prophet Muhammad or Prophet Muhammad told later as such or with additional details from his side. Mandates as mentioned above are repeated at many places in Quraan. Second to fifth pillar are also referred to as four basic duties of a Muslim.

(A) Shahaadah, called as the **first pillar of Islam**—La ilah illAllah means "there is no deity but God" or there is no other God but Allah. Muhammadur rasoolAllah means "Muhammad is the messenger of God". (**Self**–English translations only states that Prophet Muhammad is a Messenger—not last messenger—of Allah. See also **33: 40** mentioned above. One of the ten commandments of the Lord in Old Testament is "Thou shall have no other Gods before me". But Jesus has come, at least for many apart from worshipping Mary. The spellings of words in the above verse are written differently by different people but the translation is similar. The Arabic name for messenger is "Rasool" and for Prophet "Nabi"). This verse also forms the first kalima (also written as kalma at some places) in the Prayer/Namaaz/Salaat.

(B) Prayer or Namaaz or Salaat/Salaah is the **second pillar**. The second pillar is the Prayer facing to Kaaba in Mecca. Wherever a Muslim may be, he is supposed to face in the above direction. This direction is called Qibla. This instruction is given by the Prophet in 624 AD (two years after entering into Medina and therefore referred to as two yrs after Hijra (emigration), represented as 2 H or 2 A. H (Latin "Anno Hegirae" or "After Hijrah". In other words 22 years after attaining prophethood Muhammad made this directive. Apparently till then, they were praying in a different direction or irrespective of direction. (**Self**—Facing to Mecca Prophet might have been told for more than one reason. Prophet got his first revelation and far more number of revelations in Mecca. He was originally from Mecca but settled in Medina and Kaaba is brought by Abraham whom Islam acknowledges. But Jews own Abraham much more than Muslims. In Quraan many times it is said "to the Allah belongs the east and the west". In fact all theists believe that God is all pervading).

In Surah 2, Al-Baqarah verse 177-one of the very important verses—it is said that " it is not important to that you face east or west but following certain other things" (mentioned elsewhere in the text).

It is obligatory that prayer has to be in Arabic at Mecca irrespective of the one's native tongue. (**Self**--This is similar to Hinduism where it was made obligatory for prayers to be performed in temples only in Sanskrit language which is considered as sacred. But this mandate was only for the clergy and not for the general public. Of course over a period of time and till today in addition to Sanskrit, devotional songs, voluntary prayers etc are done in all languages by the clergy and general public anyhow had been doing in all languages. In future also it would be so.

Many Hindus, particularly belonging to the general masses have revolted against the mandate of Sanskrit language and seriously questioned as to why prayers should be performed only in Sanskrit? Except for a tiny minority, the rest of the people are not conversant with the language. So the question of general public performing prayers in Sanskrit does not arise. However, a few may memorise a few things and recite. (In a way it is true for Muslims too. Arabic speaking Muslims are much less in number as compared to non-Arabic speaking Muslims in the world). Tamil Nadu (a state in India) government has by law, ordered to conduct prayers even by the clergy in the native tongue Tamil in the temples. Of course depending on the clergy some can do prayers both in Tamil and Sanskrit and some only in Tamil and some only in Sanskrit. Hence there can be more than one priest in the temple. India is having so many languages and people do pray in so many languages. Not only so, even the same person can pray in different languages at different times. Many NRI's (non-resident Indians) may not be able to pray adequately even in their respective native tongues and so pray in English or other languages. Even among resident Indians, so many pray in many languages irrespective of what temple it is. So people, say by praying in English or Hindi, do not feel any sense of blasphemy. (the colloquial Hindi is actually a mixture of Hindi and Urdu and Urdu has many Persian and Arabic words). Many others, often use expressions which are used by Indian Muslims in the language of Urdu (there are even Muslims in India who cannot speak even Urdu/Hindi, leave aside Arabic). Urdu is a mixture of Persian, Arabic and Hindi and some of the expressions by general public, even who are not Muslims are in accordance with Quraan/ Islam/Muslims. Most popular are—(a) Wohi hotha hai Jo manjoorey Khudah hotha hai, which means "only that happens which is approved by the Khudah/ Almighty. (b) Uskey marji key bagair pattha nahi hil saktha, which means "without HIS permission even a leaf cannot move". (c) Allah Meharbaan Ho tho gadha bhi pehelwaan, which means "if Allah's grace is there even a stupid can become a genius / or someone very powerful or a very big personality". All these expressions are uttered by many Hindus with full conviction. Of course if one digs out, one may find such parallel expressions in Sanskrit or other Indian languages also. Two examples are—(a) without HIS permission even an ant cannot bite you. (b) With HIS grace a dumb and ignorant person can become eloquent. But the point here is, many Hindus and others are happy quoting the above expressions in Urdu with Islamic touch and they believe in it. Matured people know that God is one—call by any names and our prayers are received by the same one. One cannot conceive that God has language barriers and prayers in different languages will not be acknowledged!! The native language of Muslims across the world is not Arabic. The obligatory prayers they may do in Arabic but otherwise their voluntary prayers and ventilating themselves will be in their native languages. Even among Christians the languages are so many. God himself preached in different languages to so many prophets and the existence of numerous prophets is acknowledged by Islam too. In India, Christians do conduct their Holy Mass in native languages and other prayers and rituals. Jesus did not preach in English but the English speaking countries do their religious activities in English and similarly other countries in their own languages. So God cannot have a language barrier. And so, more than the language it is the devotion that matters.).

(**Self**- In India, if something is to be done in the language of Sanskrit, the services of specific people are solicited. However, it happens so in very little number of situations but not in the day-to-day life. In temples—not in all-priests trained in rendering prayer in the language of Sanskrit can perform the worship on one's behalf besides they doing so for the God on their own at specific times. When worship is done on one's behalf it is that particular person who is supposed to be acknowledged/ blessed by God.

Muslims mention of 99 Names of Allah which reflect the attributes of Allah. Most important thing to be understood is neither Hindus nor any other theists of other affiliations deny these attributes for the supreme. They all, whole heartedly accept the above 99 attributes to the supreme they consider. Though 99 names are mentioned, there seems to be no unanimity neither about the sequence nor the actual names in the list and not even in the total number of names i.e. some may even say that there are more than 99 names. Of course, 99 is more popular. Not all these names are mentioned in Quraan. Some names are from other sources like Hadith, oral tradition etc. But majority (81) are supposed to be from Quraan. Of course some are mentioned both in Quraan and Hadith. An important point to be noted is, this 99 includes the name of Allah. Another important point to be observed is, in the list the name of Allah need not figure as the very first name! The name of Allah may be mentioned down the list. Further it also appears that the number can be much more than 99. However, these 99 names neither form a part of the obligatory prayer/ namaaz nor is otherwise obligatory to be recited even by clergy in the day-to-day worship of Allah.

The glories of the Lord are indescribable. Hence nothing to be surprised—rather to be praised—if anyone comes out with a bigger list. Quraan itself says "If all the trees in the earth were pens and the seas with seven more seas to help it (that is the seas becoming ink), the words of Allah cannot be exhausted". (Surah **31:** Ayaat (verse) **27**-Luqman/Lukman). So the number of names of Allah in principle can increase further from 99.

Hinduism and presumably all religions/theists absolutely agree to the above mentioned 99 attributes and what all that has been said about the attributes of the Allah in Quraan. Since the languages in the world are many one may refer to the supreme and His attributes by different names. All the glories/attributes of Allah/God are usually broadly reduced to just three—Omnipotent-Omniscient—Omnipresent and this is accepted by all groups. In Hinduism attributes of God are mentioned in numbers of 108, 1008, 300, 1000 etc., 108 and 1008 being more popular. So another point (a random coincidence?) is Hindus seems to have a fancy for the number "9" or some other significance which we do not know for number 9. So the Hindu praises mentioned above 108 and 1008 can be reduced to the number "9"—1 + 8 =9. Number 99- names of Allah- also can be reduced to "9"—9 + 9=18 = 1+8 =9. May be Muslims then also had a fancy or some other significance which we do not know for number 9. Not only custodians of the culture /religion but even the educated rational theists from all social groups acknowledge the attributes of Allah mentioned above).

For vast majority among the general public it is difficult to memorise the above and chant. So a person's assistance—priest in a temple or non-priest but who has memorised-is taken to chant the above number of names on behalf of the devotee.

Though priesthood is banned in Islam, some clergy or any other person who is well versed-can copy the practice as it occurs in Hinduism without any feeling of violating Islam. Say for example the 99 names of Allah in Arabic, may not be possible for all to memorise and tell their meaning. Hence one may solicit the services of those who have memorised the names and chant the same to Allah on one's behalf. In fact not all cannot recite Quraan but those who cannot, simply listen to those who can and this practice is very much followed in Islam and is not considered as a violation of Islam. So it should be so with the recitation of 99 names or performing other rituals on behalf of someone who cannot because of genuine reasons. Hindus treat this practice as a way of increasing the number of persons preserving the ancient knowledge and making the people also to resort it more often as a means for getting blessings of the God as the recitation is done on behalf of them. Priesthood is banned in Islam. But this act need not be considered as priesthood but only as a facilitation. However, someone called "clergy" are there in Islam who supervises the society from time to time. This clergy can without any feeling of violating Islam recite the 99 names of Allah in Arabic on someone's behalf. The same thing may be done with respect to Quraan—either entirely or partially- by any one by soliciting the services of those who have learnt the recitation of Quraan in Arabic. The above may be treated as voluntary spiritual exercises for individuals–not just on specific occasions like Ramadaan but also throughout the year whenever a person feels like. Many may resort to it if so recommended by the relevant custodians of Islam. This will bring some mental peace to the persons concerned).

Praying five times is recommended or obligatory ? It appears, it is obligatory. And this directive Prophet has given in his tenth year of his prophethood (Prophethood year is in 610 AD when Muhammad was 40 years old) after returning from heaven. The ascent to heaven via Jerusalem is referred to as Shab- e–Miraj. So from 610 to 624 AD (2 AH), Qibla (facing towards Mecca) was then not apparently mandatory.

If you pray more number of times is one violating ? Voluntarily a person can pray any number of times, in addition to the prescribed number. And it is also not necessary in voluntary prayers that one pray in a defined manner and defined words. There seems to be six different kalimaas. While all the six kalimas are recited by a person in some Muslim countries it does not seem to be so in all countries. While all kalimas affirm that Allah is the greatest they differ is some other details. For example, three of the six kalimaas do not mention that Muhammad is the messenger. And three kalimaas are of supplicatory and/or praising the attributes of Allah. The above mentioned one is the shortest and is called kalima tayyab. (mentioned above as the first pillar of Islam). Al-Faatiha the opening chapter of seven verses also is recited. Further there are other additional components of the Prayer which one has to perform. (As I understand the situation in India, the person may spend a time of ten minutes for the entire Prayer, each time. So on an average one spends 50 minutes per day in Prayers. According to one Islamic posting the recommended way of each prayer varies slightly and hence the duration and so it may come to around 75 minutes a day). Though the number is prescribed and the times are prescribed viz; dawn (subh or fajr), noon (dhur), mid afternoon (asr), sunset (maghrib) and nightfall (isha), the prayer times are flexible. If you miss one time one can compensate it by praying at another time. Mid prayer is recommended not to be missed. Mosque (Masjid) is only recommendatory but not mandatory. One can pray at any place but have to face towards the west/facing towards Mecca. **4 :101 to 103**—In times of travel and war some flexibility is sanctioned by Quraan. One can shorten the prayers. Secondly, one can pray in any posture, standing, sitting or even laying down on your sides. But when at peace one has to do regular prayers in the regular manner. (**Self-** In Hinduism only in temples a fixed number and times of worshiping/propitiating the God/idol is prescribed but the general public can do like Muslims at any time and at any place and any number of times. In modern times all stress management books recommend prayer. So the person prays as and when he feels stress and even otherwise to prevent the stress affecting him. In this stressful world praying as frequently as possible even for a minute probably can overcome the stress of an individual. Even psychiatrists recommend prayer). While other prayers are flexible, Friday noon prayer is supposed to be in a group and in a mosque.

(**Self-**Something equivalent to massive gathering at Mecca is the Kumbh Melas in Hinduism which occurs not at one place but at four different places,-not every year- but once in every twelve years at a given place. At least once in a life time Hajj is recommended. Probably similar to the above recommendation in Hinduism is that one should perform a pilgrimage to Kaashi (Benares/Vaaranaasi) in India. But again it is not followed by everyone. However, Hindus have made a provision of making available and selling the water of the river Ganga which flows in the above place (Considered as Holy by Hindus) in copper vessels- a genuine concern for the people and/or a commercial venture when this was started and thus it is available to everyone without visiting the place. Muslims can follow this idea by selling the holy water of Zamzam in appropriate vessels. It will be a big enterprise. Not only Muslims even non-Muslims may purchase it).

(C) Zakat—paying an obligatory tax is the **Third Pillar of Islam**. This instruction is given by the Prophet in 624 (two years after entering into Medina and therefore referred to as two yrs after Hijra (emigration). In other words 14 years after attaining prophethood Muhammad made this directive. Of course zakat is mentioned in Quraan much before this year. The directives of Qibla and Zakat were given in the same year apparently. Zakat amounts to 2.5 per cent of one's income from all the sources. This can be paid at any time but recommended to be paid in the month of Ramaadaan when people undertake fasting for the whole month. However other details/explanations of Zakat seems to vary though not mentioned in Quraan. Obviously some other custodians of the religion are deciding it. It is also said that one need to pay a tax only if one possess more than a fixed amount of wealth which is called "Nisab" and is equivalent to three ounces of gold. Apparently this limit has been changing over a period of time. As of June 27, 2016, Nisab is estimated to be $3921.85—apparently US dollars-. However it is clear that such a limit cannot be applicable to all Muslim countries or all Muslims residing in other countries as their economic status can be very much different. Something like the income tax in modern times which is different in different countries and even in the same country it varies from time to time and people below certain income are exempted from paying income tax. This limit is again can vary as above. Secondly, Muslims residing in those countries where they are paying income tax as per the respective countries laws, should they be exempted from paying Zakat? I do not think there is any official Islamic statement about this. Of course one can argue. Hindus and others even after paying income tax they do spend some amount depending on their capacity towards religious/ charitable activities. In the same manner Muslims also can spend and are in fact spending—and this stipulation should be by the religious custodians accordingly recommended. In olden days there was no such income tax and so 2.5 per cent zakat is acceptable. But now the situation is different. I did read that for the income from natural sources—regarded as Allah's grant—example -oil and gas reserves of Arab countries fall under this category—the zakat is 50 per cent. Wealth accumulation by Haraam (by forbidden means) is sinful and one can get rid of the sin only if one donates the entire amount so earned.

In the present days it is very common for people not to reveal their real income but show less and thereby avoid paying more taxes to the government. But a real devotee should decide about paying at least Zakat/charity as per one's real income. In olden days women were not working and earning. So the question of they paying Zakat did not arise. It is also not clear from Quraan whether women also have to pay zakat. But in the present times women also go for work and earn. Should they pay zakat? There is a little confusion about this in the English translations of Ayat **33: 33**. In this Ayat it is written that women also should pay the poor the due/zakat. Paying the poor the due and zakat are they synonymous words ? Probably not. Even a woman who is not earning may donate some money or goods to the poor given to her by her husband or father etc. As the immediate preceding ayat **33: 32** is addressed to wives of prophet one may infer that even wives of prophet have to pay the poor the due/zakat!? Even when prophet had to pay Mahr (Bridal money) maybe prophet's wives also have to pay the poor the due/zakat ! A little more clarification is required for the above verses.

How zakat is supposed to be utilised? As per Quraan/prophet it is used for Philanthropic purposes (say poor, orphanages etc), religious purposes and for running the state. In what proportion it should be so spent is not clear. Apparently it is the discretion of the contemporary custodians of religion. But in those Muslim countries where there are no poor the question of expenses towards taking care of poor does not arise. So is there anything wrong if one expects that, the Zakat received in such countries should be utilised for poor Muslims in other countries where they are in need of ? Is it not a pious act ? Say, Muslims in black African countries. They are badly in need of help. Of course some other countries too. Is it happening? If so to what extent? Apparently something more can be done.

(D) Fasting (also called Saum or Roja) during Ramaadaan, (Surah 2, Al-Baqarah verses 183-188), the ninth month of Islamic calendar. (In India, it is called as Ramzaan in many places)—It is the **fourth pillar of islam**. It was made mandatory by prophet only in 624 AD i.e. in the second year of Hijra or migration to Medinah from Mecca. In other words it was recommended by prophet in the same year as that of prescribing Qibla and Zakat, 14 years after he got the first revelation! (**Self**— Is fasting mandatory? Yes. But there are exemptions. During periods of illness, journeys, old age fasting is exempted. Children are not mentioned in the Quraans but by tradition they are also exempted. And as to what age they should start observing fast may be debated. Probably it can be best decided by the parents by judging the ability of their children to undergo fast preferably in consultation with the Doctors. (remember the merciful condonations of Allah mentioned above). Ayat **46:15** (Al-Ahqaf) and foot note 4791 of Medinah (Saudi) Quraan states that "The age of full strength is held between 18 yrs and 30 or 32 years for men". So the minimum safe age for fasting may be 18 yrs if that person is normal and does not have any other problems. No such statement is made for women. Other cases mentioned—not in Quraan but elsewhere—are pregnant women, women who are to feed their babies and women in menstrual periods. (**Self**—We do not know whether any more exemptions will be added in future by the custodians of the religion, for example, medical complications. In the present times even genuine persons should consult a doctor (s) to take a decision on fasting irrespective of the age.)

Can one involve with wives during Ramadaan ? Answer is both YES and NO. From dawn to night, not allowed as it is with eating and drinking. The duration of the fast is 29 to 30 days from the beginning of the month. (The number of days missed in fasting for any reason mentioned above, may be compensated subsequently) At the end of the fasting period—as decided by the sight of the crescent moon; hence may vary from place to place by a day (29-30 days)—the festival, simply said Eid or Eid ul-Fitr is celebrated. This coincides with the first day of the next month Shawwal. (Surah 2, Al-Baqarah verses **183-188**).

(**Self**—Though the number of days for fasting is prescribed, probably there is a need to prescribe the number of hours of fasting in a day because the length of the dawn to sunset time varies in different parts of the world and according to the season in that particular place. It may vary from 11 to 16 hrs and even 22 hrs. The custodians should ponder over this—better in consultation with the doctors—in the interest of the well being and productivity of the fasting people. When the day time varies widely it appears one can follow the day times as they are in Mecca. One may ponder as to why this month has been chosen for fasting? There can be more than one reason. Muhammad received his first revelation in the month of Ramaadaan. Secondly, this month was probably considered sacred by people even before prophet.

(**Self**—Can wars be fought during the month of Ramaadaan? Yes. If need be. But during war it is difficult and is unwise to keep fast and there is a fear of losing the war. So probably it is exempted during war, rather should be exempted. During Prophet's time itself the battle of Badr was fought in the month of Ramaadaan and in the modern time in Afghanistan etc. No information as to how many have fasted during the above wars. And no specific mention of war as a situation for exemption. But war is a genuine reason for giving exemption from fasting. Fasting during other times and for atonements also is prescribed).

(E) Hajj and Umrah—**Hajj—a pilgrimage to Mecca**—is the **fifth pillar of Islam** and has to be performed by both the genders. This pillar came seven years later to Qibla, zakat and Saum in 9 AH i.e. 21 years after prophethood. (**Self**- Before his death Prophet seem to have made a visit to Mecca-called as a farewell pilgrimage after his death. So only after this Prophet has apparently got the idea of making Hajj. Recommendation could be from Mecca or Medina. Though he was staying at Medinah he preferred Mecca to be the primary place for Hajj because of the above mentioned reasons. Of course, Hajj involves visiting both Mecca and Medinah. The original name of Medinah was "Yathrib" and was apparently renamed as "Medinah" by prophet.) Is it mandatory to perform Hajj? Both Yes and No. Because, if one can, one has to compulsorily perform at least once in a life time. In case one genuinely cannot then there are specific prescriptions for him. In case one cannot (a) one should send an animal offering for sacrifice which one can, say a sheep, cow or camel (b) one should not shave his head till the above animal reaches the place of sacrifice. However, an exemption is given if the person is ill or suffering from scalp problems form shaving one's head. Apparently scalp problems were quite significant in those days in that region. But in compensation for the above exemption, one has to either fast (**Self-** period not mentioned) or feed at least six persons or offer a sacrifice (probably one has to infer that sacrifice is as above, since it is not explained further).

There is a prescribed time to perform Hajj and cannot be done at any time. If a visit is made to Mecca at any time other than the fixed one it is not treated as Hajj. And the duration of Hajj is five days, from the 8th to 12th of Dhu al-Hijjah, the last month of the Islamic calendar. This is all determined by Saudi Arabia observing the moon. Though it is an annual pilgrimage as per Islamic calendar it may come even twice, calculated to be once in about 33 years. (**Important Note**—From various Google sites it appears that there is considerable differences of opinion among Muslims regarding the months and the number of months and the number of days during which Hajj can be performed. The above mentioned month is not disputed by anyone. So if such an important point can be subjective one can think of subjectivity with reference to some other points too in Quraan/ Islamic tradition).

During the performance of Hajj one has to follow certain prescriptions. Brief mention is made here (a) No sex with wives (**Self-** -This is mentioned in Saudi Quraan but not in other two Quraans, Pickthall and Darussalaam) (b) There are so many other prescriptions which are not mentioned in Quraans but stated in different sites on Google, (c) circumambulations around the shrine Mecca called Tawaf. Muslims go around the Kaaba (the most sacred site in Islam) seven times, in a counter clockwise direction. The circle begins from the Black Stone (*al-Hajar al-'Aswad*) on the corner of the Kaaba. Muslims are allowed to kiss or touch it. If this becomes not possible they can simply point or hold up their hand to the Stone on each circuit. They also utter each time they approach they approach the kaaba, *Bismillah Allahu Akbar* which is called Takbir prayer (meaning, In the name of

Allah and Allah is the greatest). Tawaf maybe done more than once and recommended at least twice once as part of the Hajj, and again before leaving Mecca. (d) Tonsure or cutting the hair short has to be done. For women only cutting only a small portion of the hair.

Another controversy is that of performing pilgrimage by spending one's own money. Recently Pakistan has stopped financial assistance to Hajj pilgrims saying that, Hajj should be performed with one's own honestly earned money. There does not seem to be any firm declaration about this around the world. However, it is only stated that one should perform Hajj if one can afford. And exemptions are apparently there for those who cannot perform Hajj for any reason as mentioned above.

An important prohibition during pilgrimage—Hunting is prohibited during pilgrimage. However, if one does, some atonements are prescribed.(**5 :1 & 95**). But for those who does the pilgrimage by sea route hunting of fish and eating them is permitted; **5 : 96 (Self-** Though it is not clear probably in addition to fish other forms of edible sea food also are probably permitted).

Another pilgrimage which is less formal and can be performed at any time during the year is called Umrah. Rituals are similar to Hajj but lesser. Five day duration is not obligatory. And most important is that it does not constitute a pillar of Islam like the other five. Umra and Hajj can be combined with certain stipulations.

Twelve months of Islamic calendar are known as Muharram, Safar, Rabī-al-awwal, Rabī-ath-thānī, Jumādá al-ūlá, Jumādá al ākhirah, Rajab, Shabān, Ramadaan, Shawwāl, Dhū al-Qa'dah, Dhū al-Hijjah from first to 12th month respectively. Islamic year has 354 or 355 days. The current Islamic year is 1438 AH. In the Gregorian calendar, 1438 AH runs from approximately 3 October 2016 to 21 September 2017. (**Self**- it is also to be reflected as to why Islamic calendar starts from the year of Migration of Prophet to Medinah. In fact prophet did not seem to have migrated voluntarily but because the circumstances were not favourable in Mecca at that time. Of course, subsequently from Medinah he came to Mecca and conquered it. Other genuine feelings/ reasonable imaginations of people could be, Islamic calendar could have started from the year of first revelation by Gabriel to Prophet or the year of ascending to heaven from Jerusalem—Shab-e-Miraj).

(**Self**—Many other religions particularly Hinduism practices circumambulations. There is considerable variation and freedom for circumambulations. Similarly so for tonsure. Within India there is a lot of variation the way tonsure is practiced both in Hinduism and other religions too. In the modern times, just for fun many get tonsured in many places! Apart from tonsure and complete removal of beard and moustache, people for fun or craze adopt so many different hair styles and beard styles and a combination of both, many of which are imported from west. It appears that injunction—anything mandatory—regarding hairstyles, beard styles and moustache styles is not there in Quraan and it is not something considered sinful if a particular pattern is not followed and one will be punished for the same after Qiyamat. We find even among Muslims with variations in the above across the world including the Arab countries. Similarly dress code also has changed with time even at the same place. So these things are apparently trivial compared to the spiritual practices of the individual. It is evident from the above that four pillars of Islam—all four basic duties of a Muslim—have been prescribed by Prophet Muhammad while in Medinah. First pillar which is a fundamental tenet of Islam, its date is not clear. But probably one is not wrong if one infers that the concept of first pillar, Prophet Muhammad was having much before emigration to Medinah i.e. it was there in Mecca as He was getting revelations for at least 12 years in Mecca. (**Self**—Five times prayer prescription is definitely after Shab e Miraj and is not disputed. So for other pillars one may have some alternative thinking. But there does not seems to be any dispute about the recommendations of the other pillars from Medina).

In addition to the above five pillars, basic tenets and beliefs are also expressed in different verses in different Surahs.

Chapter - 3

As mentioned above in addition to the above five pillars, the other prescriptions (do's and dont's)/basic tenets/basic beliefs in Quraan/ Islam are expressed in different verses and in different Surahs. Prescriptions and beliefs even for the same issue are mentioned in different Surahs. Here again there can be more than one way of discussing. I start my discussion keeping the First Surah-Al-Fatiha (The opening) and a specific Verse-177- in Surah 2 Al-Baqarah.

(A) First Surah-Al-Fatiha (The opening) is considered as the essence of Quraan. This does not mean that a summary of Quraan is given in this Surah nor any mention of all the basic tenets of Quraan. Not even the five pillars of Islam are mentioned. The Surah has just seven verses and is considered as one Surah revealed as a whole. Another such Surah revealed as a whole is supposed to be Surah 110- Nasr (Succour/help). Al-Fatiha is recited in the daily prayers. Obviously the terms used in these verses are of the highest significance and they represent umbrella terms and expressions which need to be further expanded. And this is done in the other portions of the Quraan. In this Surah one praises Allah mentioning HIS major attributes, Viz; that HE is the Lord of the worlds, Beneficent, Merciful and the owner of the last day of judgement and fervently pleads with HIM to show the right path as prescribed by HIM and not the path which people follow disregarding HIS prescriptions and incur HIS anger or get lost their way.

The verse 177 in the Second Surah, the longest one in the Quraan gives the essence in an elaborated way specifically mentioning as to what is expected from one. It says " **It is not righteousness/important that you turn your face to east or west** but he is righteous who (a) believes in Allah, (b) believes in last day of judgement, (c) believes in scriptures (books), Angels and Prophets/messengers, (d) gives wealth to the kin, orphans, needy and needy wayfarer (travellers on foot), (e) gives wealth to release the slaves or who releases the slaves, (f) pays the poor what is due to them, (g) keep up promises they have made, (h) remains patient in adversity and in times of stress, and (i) living in one's means honestly earned. People with the above qualities are considered to be the people of truth and God fearing. (**Self**- Really a great verse and messages! I sincerely feel that people of all religions agree with the points mentioned. Six points-"d" to "i"- all religions-including atheists/agnostics etc. (Lamazhab/Dahreeya)—will agree/will have to agree *in toto*-100 per cent. This group is referred to in global census as "unaffiliated" and they constitute the third largest group in the world, after Christianity and Islam. Islam uses the word Kaafir (infidels/non-believers) for those who are non-Muslims. But one should keep in mind that all Kaafirs are not Lamazhabs/Dahreeyas. In other words many Kaafirs and Muslims can be grouped under the term "theists". As theists even the non-mulsims agree to one God, i.e. they are also monotheistic. They may call God by any name. But the above points will be totally agreed by them. For three points–"a" to "c"-they may differ in their terminology and some details but essentially all will believe these three too. So what is important to note here is what all else is not specifically mentioned in this verse ? In case this verse is made a little longer it would really give the essence of Quraan. In addition to the above this Surah discusses so many other prescriptions. Belief in Allah and Zakat has been discussed above under the five pillars of Islam. Another basic tenet of Islam-the last day of judgement is discussed below.

(**Self**—In Bible—old testament—we have in short, the ten commandments (called Decalogue)- which in a way is the most important prescriptions to be followed. They have been mentioned at two places in Old Testament—Exodus 20 and Deuteronomy 5. In a way these also constitute the essence of a human conduct. These ten commandments are supposed to have given by the Lord to Moses. **Decalogue**—(a) Thou shalt have no other gods before me. (b) Thou shalt not make unto thee any graven image. (c) Thou shalt not take the name of the Lord thy God in vain. (d) Remember the Sabbath day, to keep it holy. (e) Honour thy father and thy mother. (f) Thou shalt not kill. (g) Thou shalt not commit adultery. (h) Thou shalt not steal.

(i) Thou shalt not bear false witness against thy neighbour. (j) Thou shalt not covet neighbour's house, neighbour's wife, neighbour's servants, animals, or anything else. The language i.e. the words chosen to state the commandments can be different in different versions of Bibles. These commandments again are of universal appeal with some differences. Quraan acknowledges them, though they are all not mentioned at a single place. When these commandments were made—as in other portions of the Bible—the term Allah is not used but only the terms God, Lord, Lord God, Holy father, YAHAWEH, JEHOVA etc. Prophet has not approved Sabbath day of Jews. Point "e" is one of the important sayings of Hinduism, but apparently in Abrahamic religions God comes first followed by the parents but in Hinduism parents status has been much elevated and they come in sequence first followed by the teacher/prophet and then the God. Some subjectivity may be there with some commandments.).

(B) Qiyamat/Last Day of Judgement—Also referred to as the day of resurrection of souls or rising of all the dead, when the world is coming to an end. This is called as Qiyamat in Islam. Apparently a long time to go as per either in Islam or in Christianity or in Judaism. But anyhow it is something to be happened all of a sudden. On this day every person is judged and is told about the person's deeds when the person was alive and accordingly punished or rewarded. On this day no person other than the Allah has any power. As to when this day will come and how far we are from it we do not know. But anyhow it is something to be happened all of a sudden. But some signs of coming of that day are mentioned not only in the specific **Surah 75- Qiyamat-** The resurrection, but also specifically in at least five other Surahs. The description of the coming end is described in more details and in different ways. Here it is given in brief. Many of them are broadly grouped under **"collapse of the solar system".** The major signs are: one's sight is compounded/dazed, moon is eclipsed (darkened), sun and moon becomes united/joined together, the stars are put out/ dispersed/darkened, heavens become apart, sky looks like a molten metal brass, overflowing of seas, severe earth-quakes, mountains blown away and crumbled to dust and the respective places becoming even. Every one on that day will be bothering about themselves without bothering about their kith and kin or friends etc. Another important sign is the blowing of Trumpet twice- once before the Qiyamat when all will swoon and die (except those whom Allah has exempted) and once on the resurrection. At that time Allah is the only refuge. The sign that one's sight is dazed and the above mentioned statement that "Allah will exempt some from dying" gives a feeling that there will be some who will be left to see/till the last day. Very likely at that time so many people of all age groups would die. We cannot guess what would be the population then and what/how will be their fate on the last day or after the last day?

(**Self-** Now the important question is, how a person would be judged ? Muslim population as on today is approx. 1.90 billion in the world. According to Islam all others are Kaafirs (non-believers or those who do not follow Allah and his commands). Their number is 5.75 billion i.e. nearly three times more than the Muslims. (The above numbers apparently will further increase by the time of Qiyamat) So how they are all going to be judged? Obviously God must be having his own way of judging them which cannot be based on their religion /faith. And how HE does we cannot know. How about 1.19 billion unaffiliated groups (Atheists/agnostics and related groups called Lamazhab or Dahreeya)? How God is going to judge them?. Again God must be having HIS own way of judging various categories of people in the world to reward or punish. Of course, Islam says all those before Islam will be forgiven as it is declared as the age of ignorance (Jahiliyya). Does this mean all those who have committed so many crimes and troubled so many people before Islam will be forgiven and go unpunished ? Islam acknowledges all the Prophets before Prophet Muhammad. So people before Prophet–all over the world—would be apparently judged by the God whether they have followed the instructions given by their respective prophets or not. It appears this is true not only for the past but can be true in future too. **Surah Yunus (Jonah) 10: 47**—says " And for every nation there is a messenger. And when their messenger cometh (on the day of Judgement) it will be judged between them fairly and they will not be wronged. Apparently everyone will be judged according to their respective messenger's preachings. At the time of Prophet the number of nations were different. Secondly, we do not know how many and which nations were really meant by Gabriel? Now we have 234 nations plus territories. Further there is a long time to go for the last day of judgement. So there is every possibility of many messengers/Prophets to be there. As mentioned above **3:14** also says that "many messengers were there before Prophet Muhammad" and many prophets too since Adam. We do require great people/elevated souls to guide us intermittently till Qiyamat. Such people have to be born. You call them anything. Messenger or Prophet or elevated souls etc. Now how about after Prophet Muhamamad? If he is the last messenger apparently it means he is the last messenger till Qiyamat (The last day of Judgement) as no other prophet is going to come as per the belief and assertion. (**Self**—A distinction to be noted as per Islam is, a prophet need not be a messenger of God. Hence **all messengers are considered as Prophets but all Prophets are not considered as messengers** as they have not received direct revelation from God. However, a prophet has to be an elevated souls and apparently have God's grace. Otherwise how can they be elevated souls? Can people survive till Qiyamat without any messenger/prophet to guide them? Even after prophet Muhammad 1407 yrs have passed away since he attained prophet-hood and 1385 years have passed away since his death. As Prophet Muhammad was getting revelations almost till the end of his death, the complete version of Quraan is said to be really complete only around the time of Prophet Muhammad's death. Obviously even during the life of prophet many were not aware of the entire Quraan -as it was revealed in stages—and so many might have died during that time without knowing and following all the prescriptions of Quraan. How they would be judged? Islam says all those before Islam will be forgiven as it is declared as the age of ignorance (Jahiliyya). In view of the above fact, what exactly it means? Which year it refers to? When Islam is considered to have come? Even in Mecca and Medina this question can be controversial. Does this refer to year 610 when Prophet got the first revelation? Or 623 when Prophet died? Or when the Prophet officially started preaching Islam ? It seems when Prophet started preaching Islam he had about 70 followers only and then it spread. So even in Arab belt the time when Islam has started varies. And in other countries of the globe where Islam spread the time of starting of Islam can be considerably different. So in all these countries–the period of Jahiliyya is different—and all have to be forgiven before the start of Islam in their respective places. (**Self**–Keep in mind the discussion above regarding judgement. As it is written in Quraan "Allah knows what is concealed in your hearts". So this is a good criteria to judge anyone irrespective of any affiliation or time period.).

Taking any of the above figure—there is a sea change in the state of affairs of the world and countries from the above time till today. And this statement is true for other religions older to Islam too. There is a sea change since their inception. And naturally there will be many more changes in future till Qiyamat, which we cannot foresee right now. So there must be somebody to guide and monitor. If there is no other messenger or prophet, God should send some elevated souls who along with contemporary committed custodians of culture would guide in the light of the changed circumstances. In fact, it is acknowledged in Quraan that messengers are sent from time to time to suit to the local circumstances for guidance. But if we say like this it contrasts with the belief that Prophet Muhammad is the last messenger but prophets can be sent as per the distinction made above between a prophet and a messenger. In that case we have to speak of only either of elevated souls or prophets and not as messengers. In fact in India many great souls who revived/rejuvenated different shades of Hindu philosophy were born after Prophet Muhammad apart from the founder of a separate religion Sikhism, and different faiths like Radhasoami satsang, (these latter two accommodates all people and are monotheistic and no idol worship for the supreme. Further like Islam they preach to earn their living honestly, render service, avoid intoxicating substances and brotherhood of man.) etc. The institution Arya Samaj founded in 1857 by an Hindu ascetic Swami Dayananda Saraswati is also monotheistic and rejects idol worship. Brahmo Samaj started by Shri Rammohan Roy also preaches monotheism. In other parts of the world also such new faiths or denominations might have emerged under the leadership of somebody. Karl Marx was not a messenger nor a theist but he was as powerful as a messenger influencing so many without himself conquering any part of the world. It is his ideology which has conquered the world.

The expression "Gods chosen people", it is Jews who think they are the one. Similarly, expressions like "people of the book or believers of the book", it is Jews who identify with primarily. Probably Jews would not acknowledge Muslims primarily for the above expressions. Islam is classified as Abrahamic religions as it also acknowledges Abraham. But Muhammad of Qureshi tribe and other tribes in Mecca at that time, are not biological descendants of Abraham. Qureshi and other tribes should have been existing either as Jews or as Christians or as some other affiliation. (The problem here is, Islam does not consider Abraham either as a Jew or as a Christian but this assertion will not be accepted by the above two groups.) In any case as Islam spread to so many other countries across the globe and people there were converted into Islam and even today the conversions are taking place, all these people cannot be classified as biological descendents of Abraham though classified as belonging to Abrahamic religions. Same logic holds good for Christians too in so many countries. Late leader of Palestine Yasser Araafat used to say to Jews "we are brothers". Because, both were children of Abraham. Abraham had two wives. First wife Sarah's born were considered as Jews and those born to the second wife Hagar were the Palestinians. But at that time Palestinians were not Muslims. What they were? Jews? Or uncategorised? Though the father was Abraham for both, mother's origin and status was different. Hagar was an Egyptian maid. So tribe of Muhammad and other related tribes and people living further beyond were apparently not biological descendents of Abraham. Further Palestinians are Shias predominantly and not Sunnis. Of course, leaders of both the groups hail from Mecca.

It is really strange that Gabriel addresses in Quraan many times "Oh! Children of Israel and spends so much time in telling about biblical characters and narrations and many beliefs of Bible are acknowledged by Islam and yet both of them—Jews and Christians—are considered strictly speaking as "Kaafirs" (infidels/non-believers though they are referred to as Abrahamic religions and as people/ believers of /for the book along with Islam. So inspite of the above commonality both Jews and Christians are relegated compared to Islam/Muslims. Not just relegated, a very surprising thing is, Gabriel asking Prophet to treat them as enemies ! Why an angel who was very much present at the time of both old and new testament should say so!? **Surah, Al-Maida(The Table spread)-5: 51**—"O you believe : Take not the Jews and Christians for friends. They are friends to one another. He among you who taketh them for friends is (one) of them." So, strong seeds of discord were sown between Islam and even the other two Abrahamic religions so long back).

(**Self**—A similar description regarding the signs of the last day of judgement is given in the Bible. Jesus spoke of false Christs, wars, famines, pestilences (epidemic diseases), earthquakes and cosmic changes of all kinds. Cosmic changes description is again similar to what is mentioned in Quraan Viz; great earthquakes, sun becoming black, moon becoming blood like, stars of heaven fell to earth, and every mountain and island will be moved out of their places. One major difference is, Bible speaks of seven trumpets. With each Angel blowing the trumpet different types of destruction takes place. Another difference is, in Bible God said that next time HE will destroy the world by fire. The present day people interpret it as an atomic warfare destroying the world. It is also not clear whether at the end, the victory will be of the Jews or Christians ! ? But no where Islam is mentioned as per the biblical version. The book of revelation which discusses the last day of judgement also speaks of re-establishing Jerusalem. If so it is not a total destruction and the world will continue. At the time of Noah, not the entire world was destroyed but apparently the floods and damage was confined to some small part of the world. May be around the regions where Noah and others were living. Some say something like that of an ark was discovered in Turkey. In any case one is justified being skeptical that the destruction did not encompass the entire globe. How about the next destruction—last day of Judgement ? In case we take into account the collapse of solar system then the destruction is applicable to the entire world. But if only other signs are taken into consideration then it is again possible that the prophecy is probably confined to some small part of the globe. (**Self**- As per scientists collapse of solar system is too far and difficult to imagine).

It is said the Sepulchres will be overturned and souls/people running towards Lord. Modern man may have some doubts. In all medical colleges all over the world dead bodies are dissected for the anatomical studies. Obviously many do not bury. So no question of rising from the grave or the reference of sepulchres would hold good for them. Secondly, because of lack of space in some places graves are allowed only for some time and subsequently removed to accommodate other dead bodies. Even in cultures where burial is the custom people may go for electric crematorium for lack of space or other reasons. In Hindus, burial is not the custom but burning the dead (except for saints). In Japan, when atom bomb was dropped many people were said to be vaporized instantaneously. Now we have many times more powerful bombs than in olden days. If there is an atomic bomb blast/nuclear war, no question of either burial or burning or sepulchres turning or souls emerging from the grave. So in these type of cases the souls have to be hovering around. In future also the above practices will continue. The possibility that even those who are buried that their tombs/grave yards will remain intact till last day of judgement is remote. So what about all these souls? Obviously at the time of preaching the signs of last day of Judgement, only the situation prevailing at that time was kept in mind and not the distant future nor the practices in distant lands. Prophet was a messenger and he was also buried. Will he also be resurrected at the time of Qiyamat? And judged by Allah? In view of his status a doubt also occurs why even prophet should wait till Qiyamat/resurrection of souls?? In view of his status, does he not deserve reaching paradise soon after his death? In fact many Christians believe that to have happened for Jesus though Muslims do not believe in this. May be some others too. It is also not clear as to how the ordinary people will be judged? Say a person may commit a sin either at the age of 20 or 30 or 40 etc. So when the person is being punished, will he be given a body of the same age and get punished—whatever may be the punishment? When a person is destined for punishment the body is given. Body of which age is given before subjecting the person to punishment? The punishment given is mentioned in qualitative/subjective terms that is saying that "it is a hell of fire for them", "they will be thrown into hell", blazing fire, exposed to fire, painful doom, pouring boiling water etc. Another statement which says that fresh skins will be given to them to punish them again gives an impression that they once again become alive and get a fresh skin to get burnt and die again and the process repeats depending on the severity of the punishment pronounced on them. So death in this world is not the final death! Since people vary a lot in the magnitude (amount and type) of sins committed in their lives, the degree of punishment for these people also has to vary tremendously.

In the world so many babies and children die. What is there to judge about them ? How these babies and children are treated afterwards ? In case people have already received punishments should not be punished again on the last day of judgement. It also means from different Ayats that when once people have undergone atonements as prescribed in Quraan, they also should/will not be punished on the last day of judgement.

For the above mentioned doubts, details are not mentioned to the extent different people across the globe must be requiring to satisfy their eagerness to know the things about the last day of judgement. Probably so in all religions. How many will be forgiven and how many will be punished and to what extent and in what manner only Allah/Almighty knows.

(**Self**—The last day of judgement is not the first time that God destroyed the world though the nature of destruction is very much different. According to Bible, God once destroyed the world by severe floods. God found even then, that man has become very wicked and so HE had to destroy the world. It is really surprising. If God found man wicked even in such old times—relatively speaking much soon after HIS creation—how about after Noah and till now ? Is man not more wicked now or in any case sufficiently wicked enough for God to destroy the world either completely or leaving a few behind like in Noah's case right now? At the time of Noah, God saved from dissolution Noah and his family members and a pair of every animal species. God asked to build an ark which can accommodate all the above and required food for all for the entire duration of flood and receding period. This is where again the modern intellectuals question. The ark according to Bible was of the dimension of 300 cubits long (450 ft), 50 cubits wide (75 ft) and 30 cubits (45 ft) height. So for the modern man even of ordinary intelligence, this ark cannot accommodate what all God wants to accommodate Viz; Noah and his family members and a pair of every animal species and required food for all for the entire duration of flood and receding period. Further Noah was supposed to see that no species multiplied during the period of floods. Obviously the species preserved in the ark were such that they can multiply in a short time. How Noah could avert it, we do not know. So there must have been some other facts which are told in a different way not comprehensible to the modern man.).

(**Self**—In Hindu mythology time is cyclical and not linear as in western and other philosophies. So the world may not be totally destroyed, though few may differ on this. As per the traditional view there are four eras in Hindu mythology—Satya Yuga, Treta Yuga, Dvapara Yuga and Kali Yuga—and presently we are passing through the first quarter of the fourth and last era (Kali Yuga). So lot of time is left for this era to come to an end. The prophecies are: virtues keep declining and reach a lowest ebb with vice ruling the land. There are also beliefs that when sin increases beyond a limit, the earth will severely shake i.e. result in an earth quake. So the earth quakes are possible even as per Hindu mythology. At the end of the Kali Yuga the supreme in some form will come and destroy all the wicked and turns as a force to re-establish all the virtues. And so the virtuous-whatever number remaining-will continue in the following new cycle starting gain with Sathya Yuga.

Hindu mythology in addition also speaks of something equivalent to Qiyamat. They call it "Pralaya-dissolution" and "great dissolution called "Maha Pralaya" respectively in Sanskrit language. Like in Qiyamat signs are mentioned which are; blazing fire, overflowing of seas, everything going out of sight, sun and moon remaining without glare etc. It is unusually long period wherein there is no activity as a result of total destruction. As mentioned above Hinduism considers four great time eras Viz; Satya Yuga (1,728,000 years); Treta Yuga (1,296,000 years); Dvapara Yuga (864,000 years); Kali Yuga (432,000 years). So in all 4,320,000 or 4.32 million years. The four Yugas keep repeating in a cycle. Now one cycle of all four Yugas is called a Mahayuga or Chatur Yuga, and 1000 Mahayugas make up one Kalpa. Hundred kalpas is equivalent to one Mahakalpa. Pralaya (dissolution), commences after one kalpa and Mahakalpa commences after one hundred kalpas. The time duration of "kalpa"–the time duration of "dissolution"—is equivalent to one "kalpa" and the time duration of "Mahakalpa"–the time duration of great dissolution—is equivalent to one "Mahakalpa". During this period only the Almighty–the Supreme-remains and rest all are destroyed. Then whole cycle repeats once again.

So an important question is, after Qiyamat / last day of Judgement will again creation take place or not ? Or once for all the world is destroyed and there is no more creation ? Or like in Hinduism creation again takes place after an unusually long time gap ?).

(**Self**—the details of the way earth is formed and man evolved are fundamentally different than what is written in genesis book of old testament which is also acknowledged by Islam and Judaism. No religion believes in evolution from animals. Only science believes so. As per scientist modern form of humans evolved approximately two lakh years ago and well developed civilisations were there even 10,000 years back. Industrialisation started only in the 1800's. So one can imagine how fast some nations have developed scientifically and became a power to reckon with and provided humans with so many modern goods and services. Oil was discovered only after 1900 and subsequently Arab power, prosperity and standard of living have tremendously increased. Of course they deserve the credit to spread Islam far and wide even before the discovery of oil and development of modern warfare. So even otherwise conquerors and propagators of Islam were stronger and superior in many aspects compared to the nations they invaded. Many developed, developing and less developed civilisations collapsed before Islam. It is true for Christianity too. Of course the present day scenario is probably different. After the collapse of erstwhile USSR many people across the world were telling that now the world has become uni-polar—meaning that now only a single power i.e. USA remains as a supreme power to reckon with. Earlier situation was called bi-polar i.e. two nations were considered as supreme –USSR and USA. Of course still the present Russia ranks second to USA. Some others have come up with the theory that there is a possibility of the world becoming multi-polar i.e. many countries would be on par in terms of their power to reckon with USSR and USA. Of course it is not yet realised. Who would, time has to decide.).

(C) Talaq (Divorce) and Polygamy: Presently, In India and elsewhere too at different times there had been and is a serious debate both by the general public and legal bodies about two issues with reference to Islam,Viz; **Polygamy** (multiple wives) and **Divorce** (called **Talaq** if divorce is given by the husband and **Khula**, if divorce is given by the wife). (**Self**—These two issues pertains to other religions too. Polygamy is sanctioned since ages as per the Hinduism laws and even now it is valid as per the religion. Hinduism for ages was following a four-fold classification of the entire society. Hinduism has sanctioned Polygamy for all. However, for two communities, it was not recommended though not prohibited. Hence some examples may be there. The other two communities particularly the Royal families/clans were having multiple wives since ages till in the recent history. So if a Hindu says the government banning Polygamy is against my/Hindu religion, he is very much right! After the country has switched over to a modern form of government and modern laws the above practices have been prohibited or approved only in exceptional cases and the rules for divorce etc are also framed as per the modern times and are decided in a modern court of law and not by any clergy).

Islam approves polygamy. Fine. But, though so many important prescriptions have been often repeated in Quraan, polygamy, such an important prescription is not repeated-in any case unambiguously. Every one quotes only the Surah An-Nisa (Women) 4:3 in support of this. That is, only once it is mentioned *that too* as a part of a continuing verse. And all who talk about, do not give an undisputable version of this verse. Though the title of this verse is Women, the verses 4; 2 and 4; 3 and some more deals with the care for orphans. And it is in this context the option of multiple wives has been discussed—but not specifically as a topic of matrimonial practices/matrimonial recommendations for a man. So this privilege is probably not to be taken in any other sense. So one may imagine that privilege/recommendation of multiple wives is given only for taking care of the orphans and not for one's own desire/pleasure. Due care for orphans takes the priority and is very much emphasised in Quraan and is supposed to be taken seriously by men. They are supposed to be taken care of till they are married and one should not rob their wealth but give them their full due honestly. Otherwise it is a great sin. Really a noble prescription. (Prophet Muhammad himself became an orphan early and this could be a reason for his considerable emphasis). To take care of orphans a man may not be able to do so exclusively by himself. So it was recommended that a man may marry more than one wife and the mentioning is stopped at four. However, it is clear from the verse that the purpose of taking due care of orphans can be served even by possessing one wife and if it can be served by just one wife there is no need to go for multiple wives. The objective of recommending multiple wives was—not probably for the carnal desire of the man—but keeping in view the care of orphans and no injustice would be done to orphans. In case multiple wives becomes an obstacle to take due care of the orphans then the man is recommended to have only one wife who is not a slave or one women who is a slave. Here it can be argued whether the man has to compulsorily marry the slave or he can ask the slave to take care of the orphans without marrying her ? As the previous lines mention the words "marry of the women" it may mean that the slave has to be married, to assist in taking care of the orphans. But it is otherwise known that a man can indulge with the slave and extract work without getting married to the slave. In other words the man can take care of the orphans by the slave even without marrying a slave. Secondly, it is permitted for a man to have many slaves. So taking care of orphans without the man getting married is possible. So prescription is for marrying any one either a slave or a non-slave. Then why marrying a slave is mentioned? Is it to better ensure the care of orphans? In case the purpose is to take care of orphans then it is logical to say that it is necessary that a man has to marry a grown up and matured lady and not girls at a tender age. Now another question is, how many orphans the man is taking care of or expected to take care of? If it is to take care of, say only one orphan why the man requires multiple wives? One is sufficient. In fact, even one is probably not desirable. Because the man has to take care of the orphans and also have to take care of any children from the woman he has married. In case he has more woman at home more likely the burden of taking care of more number of children and the orphans care may be neglected. The same problem can be there even if he begets children for many slaves. So what is the best option ? Maximum one and that maximum is preferably a slave and more preferably a slave who has past the child bearing stage, so that there is no chance of adding more children at home to be taken care of. That will ensure justice and care for the orphans. As per the Indian history, leave aside an orphan, even if it is your own child and you marry another woman and bring—say when your first wife has unfortunately died-even then it is difficult for you to take care of your child! Because the lady whom you married again is called as a "step mother" and there is no guarantee that she will treat your child on par with her children. Rather she may even trouble your former wife's child(ren). A very common thing that happened in Indian history and still happens. So who is a real father? That man who after the death of his wife does not marry again in the interest and safety of his children but remains single and takes care of his children. Suppose the woman/women you bring to take care of your children or orphans does not take care of them, what you are going to do? Divorce her? Quraan says, if not pulling well admonish them and banish them. In any case the situation is an undesirable one and does not serve the ultimate purpose.

Though it is a popularly held belief that Islam does not approve celibacy (remaining single without marriage) there is no specific Ayat (verse) saying so. Of course in the present era in many places the age at which many people marry in any religion has increased considerably in spite of old practices of child marriages being prevalent to an extent.

Anyhow, irrespective of what is said about polygamy, let us take it for granted that four wives are permitted. But there is a lot to understand. Four wives are permitted but it does not mean that it is compulsory to have four wives. It is not said so. You can live with just one as well. Secondly, it also means that—at any given time—you can have a maximum of four wives. Suppose you want to have yet another one? Then, one has to get rid of one from the existing four by giving divorce and then get the fifth one, so that the prescription of, maximum of four at any given time is followed. (**But, for giving divorce the stipulations mentioned in the Quraan for giving divorce have to be followed**). Of course, there is no limit to the number of slaves/concubines/captives of war which you can retain that is prescribed. Apparently one can have many women—more than four—at the same time of all the above mentioned categories put together. In fact many Mughal emperors and Nawabs in India till recent times had multiple wives and also maintained large harem. However, **24:32** recommends to marry slaves good by nature. In other words though slavery is permitted, Quraan also recommends and appreciates freeing of slaves and marrying slaves which is considered as a good act. When once a slave is married, apparently she cannot be treated as a slave anymore and she would be counted towards the maximum limit of four wives.

A very common question that is asked is if Quraan prescribes four, how is that prophet Muhammad had so many wives simultaneously-10? Can/ Did Prophet violate Quraan? I do not think so. Prophet could not have violated Quraan but understood Quraan accordingly: that is the limit of maximum four as discussed above was mentioned only in the context of taking care of orphans and not as matrimonial stipulation or he might have considered the stipulation as probably recommendatory and not mandatory. And as mentioned above the mention four was made in context of taking care of orphans and not in the context of matrimony, though at different places the term "wives" has been used indicating a multiple number. Since in the above mentioned surah there is no mention beyond "four" it must have been inferred as-maximum four wives. However, the general feeling of the Muslims does not seem to be so. Muslims rather feel four is permitted for every one irrespective of the issue of orphans is there or not. And Muslims feel that it is a special privilege of the prophet given by Allah to the prophet and so they should not bother or they did not bother because of the esteem with which they were holding him otherwise. A confusion may arise that Prophet has been given some special privileges by Gabriel from the **Surah Ahzaab(Clans or The confederates) Verse 33: 50**. Prophet is addressed and told that "he can marry" (a) those to whom he has paid Bridal money (Mahr), (b) women who were captured in a war and making them as slaves, (c) daughters of paternal uncles and aunts (d) daughters of maternal uncles and aunts and (e) any believing women who wants to marry (**Self**— apparently there is not a difference between "a" and "e". In both the cases the women are believers. And in both the cases the Prophet has to agree and the women also have to agree and in both the cases bridal money has to be given. It may be argued that in case of "e" since the women is approaching the man/ prophet on her own, bridal money need not be given. But this does not seem to be clear.) The above mentioned have been told as a special privilege for the prophet only in the above verse. But there does not seem to be any difference between the freedom of Prophet and others. All the above mentioned relationships can be married by any Muslim. If there is/are any difference (s), only scholars have to make it explicit. Which relationships mentioned in the above suraha are meant exclusively for Prophet and not for others? And those who are doing so are violating and that type of marriages are forbidden. However, there does not seem to be any differences in the marriages allowed for Prophet in the above verse and an ordinary Muslim. Further it appears that prophet though had many wives by the end he did not marry all from the relations mentioned in **33:50**. Whom not to marry and forbidden marriages—are mentioned in **Surah Al Baqara (The Cow) 2: 221** and **Surah An-Nisa (Women) 4:22 and 4:23**—These verses though not specifically addressed to Prophet, apparently seem to apply both for prophet and others.

The above two verses **4:22** and **4:23** mentions the relationships/ women with whom one should not enter into marriage. Apparently such marriages were taking place before the revelation and all such marriages in the past have been forgiven. So by the above prescription a lady also is simultaneously told whom she can or cannot marry. However, a prohibition has been dictated for Prophet's wives in **Surah Al-Ahzaab, 33: 53.** Though widow marriage is sanctioned by Islam, it is not sanctioned for prophets wives to marry even after they become widows. That is a Prophet's widow(s) cannot marry again. Probably this was the reason why Ayesha did not marry even after Prophet's death, though she was still young. Any how this situation can not arise again as there is not going to be any other messenger. However, it is not clear whether women whom Prophet himself, if divorced, can remarry or not? But as per **Surah Al-Ahzaab, 33:28**, which is directly addressed to Prophet gives an impression that Prophet can divorce— rather divorce without creating any problems- if his wife asks for it and naturally they can remarry somebody else. Apparently such a situation did not arise in Prophets life. However, this verse means that all other men also should divorce their wives with all kindness in case their wives ask for it. (**Self-**Gabriel says to prophet (**33: 28**). Say to your wives that if they desire worldly life and its adornment, I will content you and will release you with a fair release and if they desire Allah (**33: 29**) and his messenger and the abode here after they can remain with the prophet. The above verse also gives an impression that prophets wives may be allowed to leave him. And afterwards naturally they can remarry. It is said that (**2: 240**) a dying man can give enough wealth sufficient to the women for one year and retain them. However, in case the women do not want this option they can leave him without any problem by demanding Khula.) In case of widows of general public they have to wait for a period of four months and ten days after the death of the husband (**2: 234**).

Further Prophet having wives many more than four, there is nothing for others to feel anything envious. Mostly he has married out of sympathetic considerations, old ladies, widows, divorcees, poor etc. So apparently Prophet had his own principles and convictions which we do not know. But those kings/emperors/ Nawabs/rich who came after him in different places on the globe may be said to have enjoyed. It is so in other religions too.

(**Self**—Scientists as I mentioned above do not believe in creation but believe in evolution. Man originated from apes over millions of years. Modern humans evolved about two lakh years ago and developed civilisations about 10,000 years back. Man started his life as a food gatherer and hunter and he was to defend for himself and search for mate. So the question the science poses is, since when the concept of family and prohibited matrimonial relations have come up? Scientists sincerely believe that for a very long time man was mating at random irrespective of relation or age. There were only two genders. That is all and it was free for the two genders to involve. So the concept of family and permitted or prohibited matrimonial relationships is relatively of a recent origin in the history of human civilisation. Apparently this concept came at different times in different parts of the globe and also differing in some details. Even today the matrimonial customs are different in different religions and also within a religion. Apparently these customs have been decided by the contemporary custodians of the society/religion keeping in view the contemporary socio-economic-political conditions. When once they came into existence they continued further and got established to different extents and again further got changed. In which religion/ civilisations the concept of family and permitted or prohibited matrimonial relationships have come into existence earlier, the issue is left to scholars. Hinduism religions believe in the decline of virtues at the end of this era—which is still far, far away—and at that time again the same situation as scientists have told as above is going to prevail, that is referring to his way of life of indiscriminate indulgence.

(**Self-**Now coming back to the issue of multiple wives. It is against the natural laws of creation to create a highly skewed gender ratio. Even an ordinary man knows that all over the world the gender ratio is more or less equal. Statistics say it is slightly more in favour of males except in a few pockets. However, even this does not dismiss the generalisation that nature creates males and females in more or less in equal numbers. So the polygamy for every man is not possible. Leave aside four - both in Muslim and non-muslim countries- even getting one wife to everyone is not possible as the number of females are less than the number of males. If somebody marries four, he is depriving at least three of his fellow men. When can gender ratio become upset ? War is one situation where a large number of men are killed and the gender ratio gets upset and a need for taking care of left over women arises. How this need is to be fulfilled will be decided by the contemporary custodians of the society. If they are not taken care of they are likely to be exploited. But as per the modern times, where we talk about women's rights, gender equality and gender empowerment, any rules concerning them have to be finalised in consultation with them.

Even in times of peace women have to be consulted for anything which affects them. Only then one can say that women have been given due status and they have not been exploited. Any quote in any religious book which states that a women has to be unconditionally obey and are subservient to men is not appreciated in modern times. Of course everyone knows the reality of the nature /God/Allah/

Almighty or whatever one may say, that men are created physically stronger to women and are relieved from the burden of bearing children and giving birth and feeding the new born. To say it is all because of the first woman eating the forbidden fruit (biblical episode) cannot be accepted in the modern times. But why women were so created probably we can never know the answer. But the advantages of the men are supposed to protect and take care of the women. That is how it should be looked upon. Thank God that HE has placed humans in a better situation than animals. In case of animals the poor female has to take care of itself in all ways. Probably there is something for Animal rights activists to ponder over in this regard. However, many animals involve only during a specific period of their life cycle-called heat period—but the rest of the time they do not indulge nor any male animal approaches a female for indulgence. So in these cases indulgence is only for procreation /progeny and not for recreation/ pleasure. But it is not so with humans. Another difference is, females have a menopause i.e. the age beyond which they cannot bear children. But males do not have a menopause. They can produce sperms even till late age. We do not know why nature has created so!.

Now, even if men are allowed to have/try to possess so many women. Does this mean the man's ability—vigour and vitality—will also increase as many times? Definitely not. A man by virtue of his power and wealth he may possess a hundred women. Does this mean that his vigour and vitality will also be increased by hundred times ! ? Definitely not. So apparently it means the man is seriously depriving so many women.

(**Self**—Another reason for the upset of gender ratios—not at a macro/national level but at a micro or local level—is men migrating out of their places in large numbers in search of jobs and joining military, leaving behind women. In population census they are there but are not physically there in that particular places. This is a different situation to be analysed by native custodians. Maybe it is resolved differently in different places.) **Surah Al Baqara (The Cow) 2: 221**—Marry only a believing women (Mumin/Muslim) slave or a non-slave but not a non-believer unless she converts into a believer. In Ayat **24: 32** it is encouraged for single men to marry a female slave (who is a believer or agrees to become a believer) if the slave is poor and that Allah would help them. Same encouragement and recommendation is given to women also. That is single women can marry male slaves who are believers if they are poor. Apparently the difference is a women can marry only one slave while a man can marry more than one.

In view of the above mentioned ayats, the ayat **5: 5** and footnote 700 in Medinah (Saudi) Quraan can be confusing where it is stated that a Muslim can marry women from the people of the book i.e. Christian and Jewish women more particularly because of the ayat **5:51** where Gabriel says that Jews and Christians are to be treated as enemies. It also gives an impression that women from the people of the book are married they need not get converted to Islam. It is not clear how the entire situation would be. However, though it is said that a Muslim man can marry women of the people of the book a Muslim women cannot marry a man from the people of the book.

(Self—Is it right to treat a believer or for that matter even a non-believer either a woman or a man as a slave? It does not seem to be generous. A general doubt one can get is, why an all merciful God approves/permits slavery? Does God allow fellow human to be treated as a slave ? Irrespective of religion, a merciful God cannot approve to treat a fellow human being as a slave. Atheists, rationalists and humanists have a good point in this. It is really painful to know the history of slavery particularly of the black Negroes. Of course though Islam approves slavery, it also appreciates freeing of slaves by the owners and such act is also recommended as an atonement in some cases of omission. In India and other countries there was a similar situation, called "bonded labour". Even today there is considerable exploitation of labour all over the world.

However, many Mughal emperors had more than four wives. Further in addition to wives they maintained harem with huge number of women. As mentioned above Polygamy is allowed in Hinduism. Hindu kings had many wives even more than four apart from adultery and affairs otherwise. To have an idea of their behaviour one may read the Book "Maharaja by Jaarmani Dass. Many kings/emperors in the world had similar behaviour. Not only kings even general public had a liberal attitude towards sex and in the present times it is true in many countries. Even women have equal rights as they demand both reproductive and biological rights, sex by consent, live-in-relationships etc and the same is legally and socially approved and no stigma is attached to anyone in many countries.

Though polygamy has been approved, it is made clear in Verse **4:129** that "one cannot do justice to all the wives in treating them equally, however one may wish to do so. But do not totally neglect anyone." (**Self-** It is very much right that one cannot devote time and energies equally to all wives. It is a fact with everyone in the world who follows polygamy. So the women (and their families) who enters into a polygamous relationship should be clear about this. They cannot complain afterwards of not getting enough attention. It is also not clear whether a man can marry the permitted four women at the same time/simultaneously or he has to marry one at a time ? If so any time gap between two marriages? Similar question applies for divorce too. But these type of questions in the present times probably arise only to a very limited extent.).

In addition to regular marriages as prescribed in Quraan other types of marriages also take place among Muslims and the manner can vary with the denomination of the Muslims. Nikâh al-mut 'ah is a type of temporary contract marriage/also called travellers marriage followed in certain denominations of Shia Muslims with certain terms and conditions. Regarding the minimum or maximum duration of these marriages people/native cultural custodians seem to vary a lot. However, as in case of regular marriages the women after the contract period is over has to remain apart for the confirmation of pregnancy and the liability of the same has to be apparently taken care of by the person who married. Other denominations of Muslims including the vast majority of Sunnis practice Nikah al misyar, which is considered as similar to that of mutah. The person who is engaging in these marriages need not be a bachelor. He can be an already a married man and probably the stipulation of maximum four wives does not include these type of marriages. It is also not clear whether these marriages should be only with Muslim women (believers) or it can be with others too. How about the children born out of such marriages? Do they belong to Islam or the religion of the women in case they can be married without getting converted to Islam? When the man goes away after annulling the marriage the woman is left behind and probably she can choose the religion for her children. Any how this requires more clarification. And as it is not mentioned in Quraan the clarifications have to come from the clergy. It is also not clear whether a person can have more than one Nikâh al-mut 'ah or Nikah al misyar at the same time. However, this is not probably so much required as the person can annul the contract after a short time and can materialise another Nikâh al-mut 'ah or Nikah al misyar afterwards. The most important point is, these type of marriages are not prescribed in Quraan. A corollary of this is, whatever that is practiced which is not prescribed in Quraan may not be considered as "Haraam" (forbidden). It is a matter of debate for scholars as to how Allah views all such practices at the end of Qiyamat. Are people going to be punished for these acts by Allah at the time of Qiyamat or not punished treating them as "Halal" (approved practices)? These practices and others which are not prescribed in Quraan apparently have been prescribed by prophet and/or the native clergy. Apparently the native clergy has lot of powers to frame laws and by corollary to make atonements too. With time the native clergy changes at all places and therefore the laws or unwritten approvals also may change at the respective places. This situation can be to the advantage of the people. So it is very essential that the general public remain in constant touch with the native clergy and maintain a good rapport.

Similar practice of live in relationships called "Nata Pratha" was there in ancient times and to some extent even today among some tribes of Indian states like Rajasthan, Gujarat and Madhya Pradesh. There was/is no intervention of any clergy or judiciary. It is an agreement between the partners who want to live and may involve some elders as witnesses. This was socially accepted and no stigma is attached to anyone involved in this practice. Similarly in the state of Gujarat primarily and in some pockets of Rajasthan and Madhya Pradesh also practice of temporary live-in-relationships were/are there among many social groups called as "Maîtri Karar". In these cases also there is no intervention of any clergy but witnesses and/or judiciary may be involved. Relationships get materialised by mutual consent between the partners after discussing the terms and conditions.

This practice also is socially accepted. In both the above mentioned cases, though traditionally this practice is meant only when both the man and woman are married or widowed but nowadays there are cases where unmarried people/singles also have started living in together. Regarding the above mentioned practices there are differences of opinion regarding their acceptance. Some support, some oppose and some indifferent.

In the present times in many societies in the world which are categorised as "socially liberated" people can either involve or live together and get separated too by mutual consent without the intervention of any clergy or judiciary. It is socially accepted and no stigma is attached to such affairs nor to the children born out of such affairs.

The above practices may or may not cause problems to the partners in case they do not beget/or earlier had children. But in case they beget children it would create a problem for them. How/who to take care of them? They cannot be abandoned. Further there can be children for the man and the woman before entering into the above live-in-relationship contracts. What about them? Cases of abandoning the children or abandoning the woman and the children are reported from different parts of the world. In advanced societies women have the freedom to avoid pregancies and abortions which are not there in all societies. And children's security also is not a problem in these advanced societies. But not so in all parts of the world. Hence there is a need to examine these cases in different places and do the required justice.

Talaaq (divorce also called as Triple Talaaq)-Another sensitive issue being discussed in more than one country including by Muslim women is, /When/how Talaaq (Divorce) is permitted as per Quraan? Even this information, many who are debating the issue are apparently not aware of. I am confining only to Quraan and not to any other sources. And like with many other issues and topics the topic of Talaaq also is discussed under more than one Surah. In addition to being discussed in Surah 2 Al-Baqara, there is also a short Surah-65- of 12 verses with the specific title of Talaaq. (**2 : 226 to 232** & **65: 1 to 7**)

(a) A man cannot divorce a wife unless she commits open immorality as per Islamic code of conduct; 65: 1 (This is an important point to be noted. So a corollary is, it cannot be simply the whims of men but it needs to be proved that open immorality has been committed apparently as per Islamic code of conduct. Even exhibiting lewdness can be forgiven if a woman repents—**4:15 to 4:17**. Apparently open immorality is something a greater offense that needs to be established if a divorce has to be given.).

(b) If you want to divorce, wait for four months before pronouncing divorce (**Self-** So an inference is, it is quite possible that during this period wife may get a suspicion that she is going to be divorced as the man's behaviour can be different during these four months and during this time the women and the family members from women's side should think of her future welfare measures. In case even after having in mind the idea of divorce, if the man is indulging with his wife as usual during the above four months it means either it is a deceit or the man has changed his decision to divorce. Only later this can be known. In case he indulges with wife during this four months then there is every possibility of wife getting pregnant and then he cannot divorce immediately but have to take the responsibility of her till delivery according to his economic status. So in case the man does not want this burden he should not indulge with his wife during the above four months. But if he does not indulge with his wife then it will be very clear to the wife that the man is going to divorce her).

(c) (**Self-** A confusion arises whether it requires any alteration in the sequence of Ayats or in understanding **2:226**. This Ayat says that "divorced women shall wait keeping themselves apart for three monthly periods. Here two doubts arise. 1. As it is said in the Ayat "divorced women shall wait"-that means the man has already pronounced Talaaq three times. Only then it is appropriate to use the word "divorced women". Otherwise they are not yet to be considered as divorced. However, in the Ayat **2: 229** i.e. in the third verse after **2:226**, it is said that if divorce is pronounced only twice then the man can take back the women but if pronounced thrice- **2:230**- then the man cannot take back the women unless some other man marries his divorced wife and in turn gives divorce he can take back his former wife. (**Self**—Does the expression "divorced women shall wait" in **2: 226** any way mean only twice divorced women but not thrice divorced? Otherwise the sequence of verses may require a change for greater clarity?) 2. Now what is the purpose of the lady remaining three months apart? This is to ensure that she is not conceived/ pregnant and is carrying the child of the man who has divorced in which case there lies a responsibility for the man. But why three months has been prescribed to ensure conception/pregnancy? In case there is no pregnancy the woman will have a normal menses and if pregnant there will be no menses. This can be known in one month's period. And it may be delayed at the most up to 45 days as per the modern knowledge of science and also of the females experience in the past. So in a maximum period of 45 days one must be able to know whether a woman is conceived or not. So why three months was prescribed? So much time is not required to confirm conception. (**Self**- In case as mentioned above before pronouncing divorce the man has to wait for four months. If at the end of these four months if pregnancy is confirmed then apparently there is no need for a further waiting of three more months). During the separation period man cannot harass her and should treat her as per his economic status. As mentioned above before pronouncing divorce the man has to wait for four months. If at the end of these four months if pregnancy is confirmed then apparently there is no need for a further waiting of three more months. Under these conditions it has to be inferred that the man can divorce even after knowing that his wife is pregnant but with the other conditions stipulated that he would take care of her till delivery. See point "e").

(d) If pronounced divorce only twice and reconciles it is fine. But if pronounced thrice he has to pay a price in case he wants to get back her. In case some other man marries his divorced wife and in turn gives divorce he can take back his former wife.). (e) If conceived (pregnant) the man cannot divorce. He has to financially support her according to his status till the delivery. (f) Mahr—the money which the man gives to the bride at the time of marriage, can be retained by her. In case the man has not paid the complete Mahr as promised but some due is pending, the man has to pay the balance to the divorced wife. In addition to Mahr any other gifts he has given cannot be taken back. (Though it is not mentioned in Quraan, I understand from some other sources that the spirit behind Mahr is that the woman can live on her own even after a divorce or death of the husband. Therefore, the amount of Mahr has to be accordingly decided and parents of the girl must be aware of this.). (g) Provision should be made for divorced women as per the economic status. This is the duty of Al-Mutaquun—The Pious (**2:241**).

(h) However, a man may divorce a woman without giving any time gap in case he has not touched the woman. (Surah al-Ahzaab-The Clans, **33: 49**). Apparently this means this divorce should be before the consummation of marriage. If divorce is given after consummation of marriage after the bride has gone to man's home, then others may not believe that the man has not touched her. It is also possible that the man had touched her like any other husband but could not have sexual relations because of some defect. How to explain such a situation? Is time gap required in these cases? How such a woman would be categorised? Can a man give a divorce soon after consummation of marriage but before taking the woman with him? Nothing is prescribed for such situations. What justification is given in support of a man who divorces under such situations? Any valid reason? If it is a valid reason it must be made clear and proceed accordingly so that the annulment of engagement or marriage is justified. If such thing happens what is the status of the woman ? Is she to be treated as a divorcee? This divorce is different from the above mentioned divorce. (**Self**—In India, the word "touching" as mentioned in the above Surah is a debatable one. It so happens that a lady is married and during the first or two days and nights the man has been touching her but unable to perform sex because he is impotent. So in such cases what should we say? The man has touched the woman or not touched? The woman should be said to be chaste or not? The woman did not involve in sex with the man. Then why stigma? In such cases the woman files a case for divorce on grounds of impotence of the husband and it is granted. But she is branded as a divorcee though she has not involved in sex. That is why the parents tell the facts to the subsequent man to whom they want to propose their woman or where matrimonial advertisements are given they advertise saying "innocent divorcee". The word "innocent" reflecting that the woman has not involved in sex with the man. Subsequently it is explained to the man and his family).

(i) Surah Al Baqarah (The cow)-**2:236** and **237**—a man can divorce the woman in case he has not touched the woman and he has not decided on the portion i.e. the amount of bridal money (mahr) to be paid. In this case the divorce is apparently happening before marriage function and should not be treated as a divorce but as a cancellation of engagement-presuming that bridal money normally would be decided before the marriage function is announced. In case the man has decided/committed to give a certain amount as bridal money, then he has to give half of that committed money though he has not touched the woman. (**Self**—In fact, the girls family in the present times might have spent much more money in organising the function inviting relatives and other guests during the time of engagement and marriage. So it is reasonable to expect that the entire expenditure should be paid by the divorced man apart from revealing the reasons so that the woman and her family do not live in embarrassment in the society in future.).

(**Self-** In any case either as in "h" or "i" it is really embarrassing and may even turn out to be disadvantageous to the woman and her family. What others would think as to why the engagement or marriage got cancelled ? Is the man not answerable? Is it purely a unquestionable prerogative of a man to annul an engagement or soon after marriage without assigning any reason? However, no such privilege is mentioned in Quraan for a women to annul an engagement or give Khula soon after marriage in case she has not involved in sexual relations/touched him. In India, in many religions/faiths it is not uncommon for engagements to be cancelled and even the marriages i.e. after fixing the marriage date getting cancelled. This may happen either from the man's side or from the woman's side. Recovering money spent and recovering from embarrassment are two different things.).

(j) It is also not clear whether a man can divorce more than one wife at the same time/simultaneously or he has to divorce one at a time? If so any time gap between two divorces? Similar question applies for marrying multiple wives too.

(k) The Ayat **33 :51** can be little confusing. In cases of regular Talaaq as mentioned above, in case the man wants to get back her only in case some other man marries his divorced wife and in turn gives divorce. Then only he can take back his former wife. This Ayat **33: 51** addressed to prophet gives an impression that either the prophet can keep aside a wife without giving a formal Talaq or even after giving a Talaq he can take back her without the above mentioned stipulation. Only scholars have to clarify. Again if it is so, the situation cannot arise again as Prophet Muhammad is the last messenger. This point has been mentioned because a question can arise whether anyone can quote and interpret the above surah and follow as Prophet. If it is a special privilege given to prophet then no one should quote this as a precedence.

(k) Woman also has the right to divorce. It is called Qula or Khula. In such cases women have no right to retain the Mahr. The man apparently should not create any problems for accepting the Qula. If the husband creates any problem the clergy can intervene and get the Qula materialise. Prophet in fact recommended that women may be released without any problems and in all kindness. Though we listen a lot about Talaq, we listen very little about Qula cases. Probably women are afraid to do so or otherwise unable to live because of economic reasons and social security reasons. However, the way conditions have been mentioned in more details for a man to divorce, the conditions for a women to pronounce Qula are not mentioned. But one expects that the men related to the women demanding Qula should help the woman to get the Qula granted easily without hassles. However, as mentioned above no such privilege is mentioned in Quraan for a women to annul an engagement or give Qula soon after marriage in case she has not involved in sexual relations/touched him.

Option given by the Quraan to the female is to get rid of the man if she does not like by demanding Qula/Khula. And this is possible for women only if the women can enjoy economic and social security after getting separated from the husband. Only if this is assured a religion or any society can say that women are given an equal status.

A man should realise that any rule framed for women would be applicable to his own women, that is, his own mother, daughter, sister etc. Does he not want them to be happy and secure?

(l) Additional points related to marriage and divorce—Ayat **4:19** and footnote 528 of Medinah (Saudi) Quraan—Though widows can remarry they can marry only with the permitted relations (**4:22 to 4: 24** An-Nisaa). They cannot marry with any prohibited relations nor men who are not allowed to marry as per the prohibited relations can marry a widow (**4:22 to 4: 24**). Widows property can be inherited only by a legitimately married person. Men cannot harass women in order to get a Qula/khula and take back the Mahr. As per ayat **4:128**—If wife fears cruelty or desertion on her husband's part there is no blame if they arrange for an amicable settlement between themselves. That means it is a flexible agreement but apparently has to be negotiated by some elders and/clergy. A consoling point for women is the ayat **58:1 (Al—Mujadila)**–Allah listens to womens complaints concerning their husbands. (**Self**—Therefore, even if justice is not given to women by their husbands, Allah is going to punish them if the complaints are genuine either in this world or on the last day of judgement. Apparently on earth it is the duty of the clergy to listen to womens complaints about their husbands and help them out.). Another important point is, "even if a woman deserts a mumin (muslim) and joins a non-believer the man has to return the mahr and neither she nor her husband should be harassed in any way (**80:11**). (**Self**—This ayat gives an impression that Muslim women are free to marry non-Muslim men without any consequences).

As per **60: 10** if in a war involving non-Muslims, Muslim women come as refugees they should be protected and should not be sent to back to non-believers. They can be married and if any Mahr has been given to her by the non-believer husband it should be returned to the non-believer husband. This gives an impression that among some non-Muslim groups also the practice of giving Mahr was there. One may wonder here as to why a non-believer should be acknowledged by giving him back the Mahr. Secondly, in case the man gives back Mahr to her former husband who is a non-believer, has he to give her Mahr again while marrying or not necessary?

(m) Zihar (**58:2** and footnotes **5330** and **5332** of Medinah (Saudi) Quraan—it is a divorce practice being followed in the pre-Islamic era as per pagan customs. (paganism is still there in some pockets of the world. Need to be verified whether this practice is there.) This practice was very unfair to women as she and her children are not taken care of in any manner. A Muslim is not supposed to do so. It is clear from this that Islamic prescription of Talaaq is different and a man has to take due care of the woman and her children in case he divorces. So sufficient protection is given to women as per **58:2** and footnotes **5330** and **5332** of Medinah (Saudi) Quraan and **4:128** and **58:1.** These points women and their families should be aware of.

However, there were reports across the world where men simply abandon their wives and children without any formalities and the women are to fend themselves. Social custodians and international organisations should address this issue.

(**Self**—In countries with modern laws, particularly the developed western countries the procedure for getting a divorce—either for a woman or for a man—appears to be more simplified. One can directly approach the court and the lawyer pleads for the client. No need for any big discussion or to disclose the reasons for divorce. It is sufficient to say that because of some irreconcilable differences it is not possible to pull on together. And the court agrees to it. The problem if any arises in the distribution of property and the responsibility of taking care of the children which the court decides on hearing both sides and knowing the details from both the sides. Since the state of affairs since the beginning of any religion till now has changed a lot and may further change a lot apparently there are serious limitations to apply personal laws in any case in any religion).

(**Self**—The big shots and judiciary etc should understand the implications of simultaneously giving an approval for personal law and also uniform civil code (say particularly in non-Islamic countries). Suppose a male Muslim government servant with multiple wives dies. How does the government is going to decide to give the pension? Only to one or others too? Often on sympathetic grounds a job is given to one of the family members of the dead government servant. To whom the government will give in that family? When a man with multiple wives die simultaneously many women become widows at the same time. How to rehabilitate them in the society? Of course Islam allows all the four to remarry to different people but whether they will be able to get a deal of their choice or not is debatable. And distribution of assets of the husband can be complicated/controversial -say if different wives have different number of children).

(**Self-**As mentioned above, If certain Hindu groups start claiming that it is their age old right to have multiple wives, can the government or religious custodians deny it? As per ancient rules they need not have to take even the consent of the first wife to marry the second one and so on. In such cases also the government may face a problem as mentioned above. Except for two social groups (who constitute a minority as compared to the total population of Hindus) for the vast majority of the people, Hindu religion has allowed Polygamy. For the above two communities also it is not a blanket prohibition but highly recommendatory to have only one wife. So in a way they too have a personal law which they have ignored it and switched over to a modern system.

In Hinduism, society is classified into various groups called castes which differ in their social status. But in Islam, all are supposed to be equal. However differential treatment is very much there in Islam too though not officially/legally/religiously/in preaching. For example, in Indian subcontinent all Muslims are converts-converted after Mughal invasion. The caste system was there in Hinduism since ages. Further there are many languages in Indian subcontinent. When Hindus were converted to Muslims, people from all castes and languages got converted and their original antecedents are still maintained. Hence one group of Muslims may consider themselves as superior to other groups and so they prefer to marry among themselves. They may socialise otherwise or pray together in the same mosque. That does not remove the feelings of their original distinct identities. In addition some group of Muslims owe their descendency from the Mughal emperors and so they consider superior to all other converts. There are so many Muslim countries and countries with significant number of Muslims in different countries. And they usually prefer to marry among themselves and they have their own feeling of identity. An Arabian Muslim apparently feels superior to non-Arab Muslims. They may not treat Muslims of all other countries in the world on par with them. Similarly so with an Iranian Muslim or with a Turkish Muslim who may feel superior to Muslims in several other countries. Pakistan attacked Bangladesh because they do not identify with them or alternatively Bangladesh people want to get separated as they do not identify with Pakistan Muslims. This is the situation all over the world. Christianity also has similar problems. A negro Christian or a Muslim is treated inferior. Before conversion they were taken as slaves and even after conversion they were taken as slaves. Even if they are in their independent countries they are treated as inferior. All this is a strong mental feeling and cannot be erased so easily).

(D) Jihad called Holy War—This is said to be another basic tenet of Islam. (**Self-** Though this term is well known across the globe, the English translations of Quraan do not seem to have used the word "Jihad". Such an important concept cannot remain untranslated as such if there is no unambiguity in the original Arabic ayat of Quraan. Picthall's Quraan used the word "warfare" and Saudi Quraan mentions the word "fighting". So both these Quraans have not mentioned the word "Jihad" in their English translations. Even in the rest of the verse they have not used the word Jihad (**2: 216**). Of course Darussalam Quraan mentions the word Jihad, which apparently needs to be checked whether its translation is accurate. Secondly, the prefix "Holy" also does not appear in English translations, dictated by Prophet Muhammad in Medinah in 2 H. This is supposed to be carried out to safeguard the religion. In other words only when there is any threat to the religion. Prophet Muhammad was of the opinion that persecution is worse than being getting killed and so fight the enemy and therefore prescribed some rules (**Surah 2 Al-Baqarah, 190-194**). From the above a corollary is Jihad is only when there is a threat to religion and to safeguard the religion. But puzzling fact is that even Muslim countries have waged war against another Muslim country. In these cases there was no threat for the religion and these wars cannot be categorised as Jihad or Holy war. To justify the word "Holy" in the expression "Holy war", the war must be genuinely justified. Not any war or violence can be classified as "Holy". Such a concept is also there in Hinduism which has become very popular particularly because of the war of Mahabharata. That war was classified as "Dharm Yuddh" meaning "Righteous war" and not carrying out a "righteous war" is considered as a sin. A view similar to Islam's jihad. Further it is also said in Hinduism which reflects Islam's Jihad—"Either victory or heaven, let us fight the righteous war. Victory and defeat are in the hands of Almighty".

In view of the above, the wars between Muslim countries or within a Muslim country among them may not be categorised as Jihad -Holy war but has to be attributed to because of certain other reasons. Even in the wars between Muslim countries and within a Muslim country lot of suffering in so many ways was caused to fellow Muslims. Can believers cause so much suffering to fellow believers? Quraan states atonements for killing a believer by mistake but for killing intentionally it is a sin which will be punished at the time of Qiyamat (Surah An-Nisaa (Women)-**4: 92** and **4 :93**). For killing a hostile believer also atonements are prescribed. (as to what is meant by "hostile believer" needs clarification). In any case these situations cover those cases where killing are at an individual or concerned with few but not definitely where a large scale suffering is involved of the believers by the believers. Al-Hujuraat (The private apartments), **49: 10** states that believers are a single brotherhood and so they should make peace and reconciliation. I did read at some place that if a war ensues the same rules apply i.e. same rules which are applied in case of a war between believers and non-believers are also applied and are applicable in case of a war even between Muslims. To what extent this point is agreed upon can be debatable. No war in a Mosque. However, Quraan further states that a war can be fought even in Mosque if enemies fight. If they stop fighting then war should be stopped in the Mosque.

"War widows" and "war babies" and "war victims" were/are a serious issue across the globe. How they have to be rehabilitated? Many organisations are pondering over it. Both the respective social custodians and international organisations should do due justice for them. They should be duly rehabilitated and treated with all dignity on par with others in the society. The father of the war babies can be identified by modern scientific techniques called "DNA finger printing" in case DNA finger prints of all soldiers are kept on record. This is a gigantic task and only U.N. can initiate and materialise this.

Is fighting with disbelievers (non-Muslims) a must? 109:1-6—These verses apparently addressed to prophet by Gabriel say that there should not be any conflict with other religious groups rather there should be a re-conciliatory approach. "Say. O Disbelievers. I worship not that which you worship. Nor you worship that which I worship. Unto you your religion and unto me my religion." To you be your way and to me mine". So nothing serious against kaafirs (non-believers) is said. It is only said that they may have their own way and Muslims have their own way. (**Self**—This is perfectly fine. Let anyone follow their religion, Gods etc one should not bother. Even the Ayat **2:256** also seem to indicate a similar opinion. It says "There is no compulsion in religion. One may follow other deities." But those who reject other deities and follow Allah have a firm handhold.). A similar impression one can get from **8 :39** wherein it is said if non-believers persecute you believers fight with them but if they stop persecuting, you can stop fighting.

In the present times the nature of weapons and war has totally changed compared to the olden days. So naturally the way the Jihad is fought also can vary and this way of fighting is apparently approved by the contemporary custodians of religion. By corollary the contemporary custodians may approve new things pertaining to other issues as well. Though in every country people join military as soldiers and are prepared to sacrifice their lives, Islam in addition to soldiers in military have people to carry out Jihad sacrificing their lives. In other countries they do have what are called as "suicide squads" but they are no way/need not be related to religion.

Neither Prophet nor Jesus was born and brought up as Muslim and Christian respectively. Jesus was a Jew and Prophet Muhammad must be born into a family /tribe following some native practices of religion. Only after they started preaching and after their death the respective religions have spread. Of course the above situation is true for founders of other religions too. But Hinduism does not have any specific founder. The terms Hinduism and Hindus are not coined by the natives, but they have somehow become popular in usage both in private and official matters. Native term for Hinduism is "Sanaathana Dharma." Of the two Abrahamic religions two leaders-Judaism and Christianity were Jewish. But Prophet Muhammad was an Arab from a Qureshi tribe. And Karl Marx who influenced so many people is also a Jew.

Chapter - 4

A. (Self-Revelations/Comparisons between Jesus and Prophet Muhammad etc.)

On mount Tabor Jesus was supposed to have transfigured into an exceedingly bright form and conversed with Moses and Elijah. Whether Jesus is God or incarnation or son of God even Abrahamic religions including Christians seem to differ. Islam outright rejects all, except considering him as just another messenger. Not only that Islam and even some others from Abrahamic religions do not believe in the death of Jesus Christ by crucifixion. As per **Ayat 4:157 and footnote 663** of Medinah (Saudi) Quraan, Jesus was not crucified and apparently this is said by Gabriel himself. Further, like many others the compilers say that not much of Jesus life is known but for his preaching period which is of a very limited period 2-3 yrs and both his birth and death are a mystery. However, Islam acknowledges the Holy conception of Jesus. But regarding other details like pregnancy period, delivery etc different affiliations including Islam may differ **(Ayat 19: 20 to 19; 23 and footnotes 2474, 2475 and 2487** of Medinah (Saudi) Quraan). Hence, Islam does not approve of the Holy Trinity concept as well (God-Son of God—Holy spirit i.e. Almighty—Jesus and Holy spirit. No one can be co-equal to Allah/Almighty. Even among Christians there is no total unanimity regarding this. Hindus cannot refute anything as they accept incarnations and enormous deifying/deification).

Some comparisons and contrasts between Jesus and Prophet Muhammad-Jesus was supposed to have preached for only two to three yrs presumably on his own, whereas Prophet Muhammad preached for nearly 23 years by getting revelations from angel Gabriel. Jesus was crucified and at an early age (maximum fixed at 36 and minimum fixed at 33 yrs) while prophet died a natural illness at the age of 63 yrs. (A wild speculation could be that he was poisoned or what Prophet said was to be taken "as a figure of speech"?. According to Prophets wife Ayesha, prophet used to say in his last days "O" "Aisha! I still feel the pain caused by the food I ate at Khaibar, and at this time, I feel as if my aorta is being cut from that poison.").

Neither was a Christian or Muslim by birth respectively. Jesus was Jew and Prophet Muhammad might be belonging to some tribal faith existing then. After they became powerful personalities their followers became Christians and Muslims respectively. In other words they were founders of a new religion Christianity and Islam respectively, like Buddha (lived for 80 years) established Buddhism and Guru Nanak (lived for 70 years) established Sikhism etc.

After Jesus many Jews got converted into Christianity and after Prophet many Jews and Christians also got converted into Islam apart from so many others. And many from those before Jesus and after continued to remain as Jews. But today Jews constitute only a tiny minority among the Abrahamic religions. Jesus never married but prophet is a much married person. As per **ayat 13:38** and **footnote 1861** of Medinah (Saudi) Quraan this point was mentioned as if already determined by Almighty/Allah. It is said that "we send messengers before thee and appointed them wives and children". Apparently Jesus was excluded. This statement can also mean that Prophet Muhammad's multiple wives—in the later stages of his life—also has been determined by Allah/Almighty and so there is no violation of the maximum of four wives prescriptions as generally quoted. However, it needs to be mentioned that Prophet remained with only one wife for 25 years and only during the last 12 years of his life he married others. Jesus was believed—at least by many—that he is born of holy conception to a virgin and there were some divine announcements before his birth and special incidents after his birth. But Prophet's birth was normal like that of any body and nothing special discussed after his birth. Rather he became an orphan very soon. But Joseph had other children from Mary and Jesus had apparently lived with them. Islam does not also believe in Jesus resurrection. There is no such resurrection in case of Prophet but he was buried like any other person and so even Prophet Muhammad will be resurrected on the same day as the rest of the ordinary people on the last day of judgement (Qiyamat). But Prophet has visited heaven even while alive along with Gabriel-called Shab-e-Miraj. If resurrection is true—Easter is celebrated all over the world- then Jesus also went directly to heaven with the body but at the end of his life. Jesus performed many miracles even during his short life. Except revelation and ascension to heaven there seems to be no other miracle happened to prophet nor prophet has performed any miracles during his life. However, some Muslims do attribute some miracles to Prophet which is not acknowledged by many others including even by fellow cultural custodians and Muslims. New Testament was compiled after the death of Jesus and so with Quraan after the death of the Prophet. Though many were involved only one Quraan was compiled after the death of the Prophet. But four different Gospels of the New Testament were compiled by four different apostles who are definitely known. However, some differences can be there both in the Bibles of Christians belonging to different denominations and similarly so among different denominations of Muslims).

(B) Shirk (idolatry) forbidden and a sin in Islam. Though idol worship was common in pre-Islamic period in the regions surrounding Prophet's place, subsequently Prophet was deadly against idol worship and Idolaters and supposed to have ordered the destruction of many idols and kill many idolaters. It is really surprising that even in Quraan it is recommended to slay the idolaters (apparently said by Gabriel and not by Prophet on his own. There is a possibility of this point being confused by people). Probably it is logical to infer that when Prophet Muhammad vehemently opposed idolaters he had only idolaters around his region in mind and not Hindus and others who are far away. Subsequently the ideology was spread along with the Muslim invaders. (**Self-**Why so much of antagonism for idolaters? Is it because Gabriel told? Or Is it because it is one of the ten commandments in the Bible accepted by Islam? Just because somebody is an idolater or following some other practice we may not or cannot start killing/hating them. There must be some other convincing reason. A speculation could be, some social groups in and around Mecca and/or who have come from outside must have been troubling/exploiting other social groups a lot which includes Prophet

Muhammad's social group and his related social groups. And the exploiting social groups were presumably idolaters. So Prophet Muhammad revolted against them and also their practices. Subsequently all followers of Prophet started hating idolaters even elsewhere, because of Prophet's earlier commands. Revolt against Clergy by people, whether they belong to idolaters or not, was there in history. So the reasons for revolting can be something different. Unaffiliated groups, (atheists/agnostics etc) are the third largest group in the world. They are neither idolaters nor non-idolaters. They are against and /or indifferent towards every religion and every clergy. So the reasons for them becoming so are different. And they are not in any way troubled by any religious group even in their respective countries. Of course in Islamic Countries if some natives start saying that they are atheists they may be severely punished. As long as people do not trouble others one can be indifferent to them if not friendly even if their practices are different rather than hating them. There are some flexible and accommodating recommendations which we may consider. As mentioned earlier Ayat **109: 1to 6** says that there is no need of confrontation with disbelievers. Say to them : "I worship not which you worship. Nor you worship that which I worship. Unto you your religion and unto me my religion" and "to you be your way and to be mine" and avoid any confrontation. So one has to take into consideration the most benign and harmonious Ayats. It is said in **9:4** that if an idolator has a treaty with you and do not work against you, you should not attack them unless they break their treaty. As mentioned earlier who has created the billions of non-believers ? Is it not the same Allah ? A similar expression is given in the Ayat **6 :108.**-it says "had Allah willed people would not have been born as idolators. You are no way responsible for them and hence no need for confrontation with them".

Karren Armstrong states that "Despite the bad press in Bible (**Self-** difficult to imagine as to why Karren Armstrong mentioned only Bible and not Quraan as well? Apparently she feels that Bible is the origin for the Quraanic prescription) there is nothing wrong with idolatory *per se* ; it only becomes objectionable or naive if the image of God, which has been construed with such loving care, is confused with the ineffable reality to which it refers.". (**Self-**In fact forbidding idol worship is one of the ten commandments in the Bible. But at least Christians in large numbers (rather they are in largest numbers) do worship the idols of Jesus, Mary etc. even today and the practice will definitely continue and may even expand. Are they blasphemous / violators? They are in human /anthropomorphic form. Karren Armstrong who worked as a nun must be definitely knowing the above fact and in all likelihood does not consider the worship of idols of Jesus or Mary as blasphemous. As mentioned in the Bible "Man has been created in the image of God". So why to despise so much an anthropomorphic form or worship ? Many civilisations for a very long time, even well developed were polytheistic before Abraham, and naturally before prophet/during prophet till he disapproved, and Hinduism is so even today. It is not that Hindus are totally ignorant of the fact that there is only one supreme. All highly spiritually evolved souls believed in one supreme and acted accordingly. They know very well that there cannot be two Supremes. They know very well that the Almighty/Supreme of all the people in the world is only one though we may be refer to as differently as per the native languages. "Sab ka Maalik Ek Hai", meaning the supreme being of all of us is the same. A Sanskrit saying–"Ekam sat vipra bahuda vadhanti"–means the truth is one but great souls happened to tell it in different ways. "Allah' is an Arabic word for the supreme. In other languages the word can be different. Spiritually evolved souls even in religions who practice idol worship, were not in need of any idol for their spiritual practices. However they did worship different idols for a different reason and with a different understanding. They firmly believed in the attribute of the supreme being Omnipotent, Omnipresent and omniscient. They firmly believed that the one supreme is all powerful, all pervading, transcendental and all merciful and can manifest anywhere and in any form. But the real nature one cannot comprehend. They know very well and even many among the general public know very well that the supreme as mentioned above cannot be confined to any idol. An idol or any mind can no way describe the supreme. The supreme is infinite while any idol or mind is finite. In Hinduism also an idol / image is not absolutely necessary for worship/prayer. Like Muslims they can also pray without an idol/image in various places other than in temples and even in the temples not looking at the idol/image. Even

Muslims pray at various places other than the Mosque and therefore the surroundings of the person who is praying can be of varying nature. Apparently the person is not concentrating on the objects surrounding him but praying remaining oblivious of the surroundings. This is also true for Hindus praying both within temples or outside the temples. The terms "Nirgun"/"Niraakaar" (meaning without form) are very much approved terms in Hinduism and other Indian born religions. Worship is called Upaasna. Worship without form is called Nirgun Upaasna. God being called as Niraakaar (without form) is very much acceptable in Hinduism. (**Self**- Since God is omnipotent though HE is without form one believes that HE is capable of assuming any form and can manifest through any form). Worshipping without form is practiced only by elevated souls or those who have already grown enough spiritually. Ordinary people are recommended initially to worship with form and in case they feel they have grown spiritually they can do away with the form, that is the idol/image. In fact it is a common practice even for ordinary people to pray without looking at any idol or image. Worshipping with form is called Saguna Upaasna. For an ordinary man in the initial stages it was/is presumed that focusing mind on an object and improving oneself spiritually is an easier task. A similar feeling is also there in some Christians who justify idol worship of Jesus and Mary.

The Hindu ascetic who founded the institution Arya Samaj is monotheistic and rejects/does not insist idol worship. It is so with some other faiths in India. In a population vast majority are not highly spiritually evolved. But they too have a need to grow spiritually. Idol worship is just a way of focusing their attention and when done with sincere devotion and immense faith, the all merciful one supreme can manifest even through that ordinary idol/ at that place or bless you otherwise for your worship. The form and nature of the idol is immaterial. What matters is the devotion and belief with which one is praying. Since people have witnessed the manifestation/blessing of that one single supreme by focusing themselves on an idol they continued to do that practice. And where and how one can genuinely focus can differ from person to person or a group of persons to another group. A natural variation in the mind disposition. And it works differently for different people. It does not work in the same manner for all. As the Indian philosopher Aurobindo has once remarked- "Should I believe what other say or my own experience?" While there may be some fake, there are definitely some who were genuine in stating their experiences and there are people who honestly believe them. And they practice accordingly. An object is a psychological/an emotional need. And an object will definitely help in focusing the mind and subsequently pave the way for concentration. In Hinduism though Idol worship is there, meditation without an object is considered supreme but extremely difficult to the ordinary people who constitute the majority. Further bowing to different deities is done with faith in the saying "that to whomsoever you bow you bow to me i.e. the supreme." As Indian philosopher Swami Vivekananda said "God has been an emotional need for ages" Atheists should not suppress or indiscriminately ridicule the theists irrespective of which religion or faith they belong to. It is earnestly believed by many philosophers that, but for God and philosophy a huge number of people would be suffering from depression and emotional instability and there will be a need for a large number of psychiatrists in the society. However praying to abstract / formless either by Muslims or Jews or Christians is very much acknowledged by the Hindus and they believe that it is as good a spiritual practice as mentioned above.

(**Self**—Medical doctors/scientist do positively acknowledge trance and hypnosis but not other experiences. In trance often a person can talk a lot but how much of it makes sense can vary a lot. Brilliant/ highly talented people may come out with brilliant compositions/ exemplary outputs. It is considered as a state of an evolved mind or a superior mind or a person endowed with superior skills etc. Of course these people may simply say -Thank God i.e. acknowledge God for their output. Because they believe that they would not have been able to make such brilliant compositions or brilliant output without the blessings of the God. And in fact it is so customary to say so even with an ordinary person. Suppose something good happens many say - Thank God, it is all God's grace etc. One might have put in lot of effort to materialise that something. Yet one would say as above and it is so with many people. In the world we find so many people making so many efforts to achieve so many things. Are all successful? No. Some—rather maybe only few—are successful either completely or to different extents and in fact many fail. What is the reason? On a worldly plane one can analyse in different ways but it is quite common to say "I did not have God's grace or luck etc". Constantly pondering over something can result in a person coming out with some appealing conclusions. And constantly pondering over something can also effect one's dreams. Say if you are constantly looking at an object that object may appear in your dreams. That is how often many see in their dreams their kith and kin, friends and even the constructions of holy places etc. Because their form becomes etched in your mind which gets manifested in your dreams and you may even start talking to them and they talking in turn is not they talking but your own brain is talking! Sometimes what they have talked to you in the real life, such a conversation also may be there in dreams. The great chemist Kekule supposed to have discovered the structure of the chemical substance benzene because of a dream which he interpreted subsequently. Revelations are called "apaurusheya" in Hinduism. And Vedas (in all four in number)—compositions which are considered as primary authority in Hinduism— are supposed to be composed by listening to voices rather than by one's own self. Unlike with Quran these voices/listenings are not ascribed to any specific celestial person but are just considered celestial. And a basic difference is these listening spanned over much longer time compared to Quraan and the volume of all the four Vedas put together is much more than Quraan. Of course rationalists do not subscribe to this view but state that such compositions have emanated from spiritually evolved minds.).

(**Self**-The way in Islam prophet told—no one after me—in a way it happened so in Sikhism too. After the tenth guru (Preceptor) no further preceptor was declared and people were asked to follow the Book entitled "Guru Granth Saheb". So can book be treated as an idol or on par with a living prophet? But people bow to the book in all reverence and may express themselves in emotion at the place where the book is kept. Many do not know how the founder of Sikhism religion Guru Nanak looks like and so with other Gurus for a long time. But much latter, two eminent painters (Sardar Sobha Singh and Kanwar Singh) have made their sketches and people look them with deep reverence and keep them in their houses. It seems to be so with the photos/idols of Jesus and Mary. In fact, in olden days when photography was not there the persons image was preserved only by painters who did an excellent job and by sculptors. We do have verbal and visual depictions for Prophet Muhammad too. But I have not seen any visual paintings of him in any Muslims houses where I visited. However, many images of Prophet Muhammad, and the heavenly animal Buraq are found on internet. Of course photos of Mecca and Kaaba are there in Muslim houses. Now it is just a natural response to look at them in deep reverence and one may even spontaneously utter something to Allah. Similar thing can happen in other religions/faiths where idol worship is banned. And gradually it becomes a routine. When Muslims look at the Black stone in the Kaaba, don't they look at it with all reverence? They do. When they kiss the stone and raise hands in reverence is it not adoring/venerating a stone ? Muslims may not classify it as worshipping the black stone. But Muslims hold it in all reverence and it gets registered in the mind. A devoted Muslim can definitely recollect it both in the waking state and also in dream state. Hindus may say that the stone is being worshipped. That is their way of expression. And in English the word "worship" can be used in the sense of adoring, venerating even an object. Such acts cannot be said as sacrilegious. Hindus worship stones with and without form. Actually it is a reverence got transformed into a scale of worship.

Strangely I did come across a few Hindu places of worship where there is no idol/image. People still go there and offer their prayers and may light a lamp/camphor. Similarly in many other Indian born faiths there is no idol/image but people offer prayers either in the presence of a preceptor of the time or even without the preceptor being present or just keeping a photo of the founder or an earlier preceptor (Sikkhism , Radhasoami satsang etc). They are not worshipped in any way nor prayers being offered to them in any way. Devotees feel the offering of prayer only to the supreme.

A characteristic feature of the Muslims in Indian sub-continent is praying and worshipping "Dargahs"-a Persian or a Urdu word for tombs of great saints. (Of course it is banned in Islam proper). A large number of Muslims worship them and they have a strong belief that their prayers will be answered and a large number have already acknowledged it. At least Muslim clergy from Indian sub-continent

(India-Pakistan-Bangladesh) will not object to it. More interesting is the fact that it is not only Muslims but even Hindus go and pray at Dargahs, though they do not go to Mosques, while Muslims go both to Mosques and Dargahs as well. Muslims no way object Hindus coming here and offer prayers. Even Hindus feel that their prayers are answered at the Darghas. As the Quraan often says: "Allah knows what is concealed in your heart"; "Allah is all embracing and all knowing"; "Allah is ever hearer and seer" and so on. So whether it is Darghas or somewhere Allah can analyse you.

Similarly another characteristic feature of Indian sub-continent is to consider the number 786 as sacred. This is not approved in Islam proper. Number 786 is considered as the numerical value for Bismillahir-Rahmanir-Rahim (In the name of Allah, the most Merciful, the most Beneficient) written in Arabic. Such calculation is supposed to be derived from an ancient system of Arabic numerology called Abjad. Yet another feature which is not approved by Islam proper is "Mysticism". There is no place for mysticism in Islam. There had been many mystics in many religions. Many Sufis who consider themselves as Muslims were great mystics. And the philosophy of Sufis is widely appreciated by Hindus.

On Google many visual depictions of prophet are there. If from these depictions and from any archives or visual descriptions available a creative painter can visualise and paint the photo of Prophet Muhammad. In case they are sold as photos or paintings I am sure the nearly two billion Muslims will all purchase them and keep in their houses and look at them in reverence. Even millions of non-Muslims would purchase. A similar exercise can be taken with the heavenly animal Buraq. It is in no way can be considered as blasphemous. It will be a billion dollar enterprise. That money can be used for good purposes. Now look at the cross which is considered holy by so many and worn by clergy and even others. What is actually a cross? It was used for capital (death) punishment -to crucify people on the cross; a severe form of capital punishment. It was being used before Jesus, during Jesus period and even afterwards to crucify people. So how it became holy? Because Jesus also was crucified and so the cross became a Holy symbol or object. Before that, cross was never considered as holy. So many methods were used to kill people from ancient times till today. Sword, Guillotine, noose, gun, electric wheel chair, lethal injection etc. Can we treat these as holy? Hindus do hold in reverence weapons which can be used to kill as they are associated with some deity or other.

(**Self**-Genesis portion/creation aspects of God as mentioned in the Bible is acknowledged by all the Abrahamic religions. **Bible says –Genesis 1:26 "And God said, Let us make man in our image, after our likeness...:"; 1:27 "So God created man in His own image, in the image of God created he him;..." and subsequently He declared him a power to reckon with. "Man has been made in the image of God". So man need not be so despised nor an anthropomorphic God be so much despised. Man is the most privileged. After creating him from the dust, God breathed into his nostrils and the man came to life. What is that which God breathed in to the nostrils ? Simply Air ? Definitely not. Because it was already existing along with so many other objects which God has created in the universe including diverse flora and fauna. So it has to be something too subtle or too important. One can only imagine that what God breathed into the nostrils was nothing but "Soul".**

Hence humans are with souls. Abrahamic religions do not consider any other creatures to possess souls. And in ancient texts there is no clear mention of microorganisms which as we know today constitutes the major living biomass on earth, not plants, animals or humans ! In fact it is so with other religions too. They do not mention microorganisms though humans are intimately connected with them though not all of them. But they constitute the maximum biomass on earth. As they are considered as living the questions whether they also posses soul can arise in some).

(C) Brief Biographical details of Prophet (some details have been mentioned at other places in the text)—Mawlid or Milad Un nabi, is the observance of the birthday of the Islamic Prophet Muhammad which is celebrated in 12 (Sunni)/17 (Shia) Rabi' al-awwal, the third month in the Islamic calendar. It can fall either in November or December. Year 570 A.D. is widely accepted as Prophet Muhamamd's birth year. His father Abdullah died in 569. So Prophet Muhammad's mother, Amina, was a widow when she gave birth to Prophet Muhammad and his mother also died in 576 when Prophet Muhammad was six years old. Apparently Amina did not marry again, which is not an uncommon practice in those days. So prophet's mother took full care of Prophet and was apparently her commitment was of a highly concerned mother. So Prophet was an orphan brought by his grandfather and others.

His personal/family life is really difficult to analyse and to comment. He married for the first time with Khadija who also belongs to Qureshi sect. However, Khadija—a twice widowed- was 40 years of age while prophet was only 25 years of age. So Prophet Muhammad was the third husband of Khadija. Further Khadija had four children from her former two husbands. As to why prophet had to marry her, when he could have married any one not only younger to him but also to someone for whom it is a first marriage, is not clear. Equally surprising is the fact, Prophet Muhammad did not marry again till Khadija has died at the age of 65 years i.e. Prophet was 50 years then. So for 20 years Prophet Muhammad did not marry again, while so many during his time might have done so and possessed multiple wives as per the then traditions. This is something to be highly appreciated of Prophet. He got the first revelation at the age of forty in 610—a widely accepted date i.e. 15 years after getting married to Khadija. Even few years before attaining Prophethood he was supposed to have been listening to voices. However, the first revelation -presumably the first five verses of **Sura Alaq (The clot),** which Prophet undoubtedly felt was in 610 in the cave of Mount Hira, near Mecca and was convinced that he was a Prophet. This was apparently on 12 February, Monday 610 A.D. The revelation was supposed from Angel Gabriel (Jibreel in Arabic) This Surah however is placed in the 96th in the sequence of 114 total Surahs. Prophet Muhammad apparently waited for nearly three more years to publicly declare his Prophethood. There is a controversy as to how many more revelations he would have got during the above time gap. Some say that there had been a time gap of two years and three months between the first and second revelation while some even say it was three years. Best left to scholars for such controversies. In case there had been a big time gap between the first and second revelations, apparently Prophet had very little to preach during that period. With Prophet Muhammad Khadija had six children; four daughters and two sons. From the date of births available Khadija had five pregnancies with a difference of one to two years between some children. (**Self**- The death of the sixth and last child as a baby in 615 AD is little confusing scientifically in the present times, as a woman normally enters menopause by that age. Khadija would have been 59/60 years by that year. By that age ladies in prophet's time and even today were/ are considered as "past child bearing" age. Rare cases may be there). Another surprising fact is that Prophet lived with Khadija for 25 years and in this entire time he never married anyone else ! Reason as to why Prophet Muhammad did not marry anyone else till then, only Prophet knows. One can only make wild guesses. Probably he was lost in his spiritual retreats and revelations and more over he got his first revelation and Prophethood during Khadijas time and so he refrained from marrying anyone else for a long time. In any case prophet not marrying any one till Khadija died is to be greatly appreciated.

However, after Khadijas death he married 10 women. (some mention has been made elsewhere in the text. Further this number may slightly differ even among Islamic historians. Except two all other marriages are supposed to have occurred after migrating to Medinah). Prophet Muhammad had another male child-Ibrahim- with an Egyptian maid. All children of Prophet have died when he was alive except Fatima. However, even she died a few months after prophet. Two male children of Khadija born to Prophet Muhammad died even when she was alive. Though Prophet Muhammad had many wives he had no children alive to continue his lineage except Fatima. Ayesha for whom Prophet was supposed to be fond of did not beget any children. (**Self**—It is really a pity and one wonders why Allah has chosen Muhammad to become Prophet but was not merciful at all to him with respect to his children. Allah has snatched away all of them prematurely and Ayesha who preached Quraan for a long time after the death of Prophet Muhammad, was not blessed with any child and Prophet Muhammad was very unfortunate to see all his children die while he was alive except Fatima and bear all the grief).

Another remarkable event in Prophet Muhammad's life is ascending to heaven in 620. This is termed as Shab-e-Miraj—Isra and Miraj, also known as Al Isra wal Miraj or simply Miraj (Night Journey). It is observed on the 27th day of the month of Rajab, the seventh month in the Islamic calendar. This event marks the night that Allah took Muhammad from Mecca to Jerusalem and then to heaven. It is thought that prophet got the instruction of praying five times a day during this period. Since this is tenth year of Prophethood, apparently, nearly for ten years there was no specific command of Prayer (Namaz/Salaat) which is considered as the second pillar of Islam. The Isra is referred to the part of the journey of Muhammad from Mecca to Jerusalem. Gabriel was supposed to have come to Prophet Muhammad along with the heavenly animal - Buraq- which carried Muhammad to the Masjid Al Aqsa in Jerusalem.The present day Mosque is different from the one existing during Prophet's time.

Buraq images on internet vary and is usually is like a double winged horse with a human face (in some images it is a male face while in some it is a female face) wearing a helmet. Buraq, took prophet to the various heavens, to meet first the earlier prophets and then God (Allah). (**Self**—How long prophet was with Allah? Long back a Muslim in Hyderabad, India, said for two hrs Allah called prophet. So it is probably a common man's perception. However some say neither he nor Gabriel could enter the seventh heaven and see God.).

Due to opposition in Mecca Prophet Muhammad was forced to emigrate to Medinah, then called Yathrib in 622. This is referred to as Hijra and is considered as the first year of Islamic calendar. Before that is called Pre-Hijra period and from the date of entry into Medinah it is designated as 1. H or 1.AH, ("H" for Hijra). However, in 630, Prophet again entered Mecca and conquered it. Two more important battles were, battle of Badr and battle of Uhud in 2 H and 3 H respectively. At different periods of time Prophet Muhammad was recommending different prescriptions—do's and dont's (mentioned elsewhere in the text). The end of Prophet Muhammad came on 8th June 632 when he was 62/63 years old, which corresponds apparently to 12 Rabi, 11 H, Monday forenoon and buried a day or two late in Medinah near by Ayesha's house. His tomb is one of the important places visited during the pilgrimage to Mecca. (**Self**- There must have been some techniques of dead body preservation for some time during those days also. Egyptians preserving mummies is different from the intact dead body preservation and the dead body preservation in cold conditions in mortuary in the present times. To repeat a point once again. While for some events chronological details are given more informatively it could not be done with all the Surahs.).

Emigration to Medinah (Yathrib) in 622. According to Karren Armstrong, only in 624 prophet gave orders to pray in the direction of Mecca. (**Self**-- However Kaaba is built by Abraham and not by prophet or any other Muslim. So Prophet and all Muslims in the world are acknowledging and worshipping the Kaaba in Mecca built by Abraham. Prophet did not try to build another place of worship even after he received an independent revelation. Abraham and other biblical characters cannot be categorised as Muslims—though some commentators say they were neither Christians nor Jews. So by corollary they are Muslims which will not be accepted by Christians and Jews to by other scholars. Only those after prophet can be categorised so. In 630, Prophet again entered Mecca and conquered it. In 632, shortly before his death Prophet made a farewell pilgrimage to Mecca. Hence Hajj has become the fifth pillar of Islam.). (**Self**— So it is clear that from 622 to 632 for some time, prophet remained in Mecca and returned to Medinah. And again he went for a pilgrimage to Mecca in 632 and returned to Medinah. Since prophet died soon after the pilgrimage in 632 it is very likely that it is referred to as "Farewell Pilgrimage" later by others). Revelations were supposed to be occurring to Prophet till shortly before his death.

(**Self**-If prophet emphasised just and equal society, brotherhood and social justice, even the modern societies all over the world are demanding it. But relatively rich and poor cannot be eliminated. Even rich Arab nations have kings and other sheikhs who are much better off than the other Arabs. However there may not be any one suffering from poverty or basic needs and enjoying a minimum standard of life. In other Muslim countries even this is not so. There are vast differences).

Shariah law came much later to Quraan. This is supposed to be based both on Quraan and as well as prophet's advise and recommendations. So it would be an useful compilation—another great book sale- if these two components can be separated and published. How much of shariah law is based on Quraan and how much is based on prophet's sayings/approvals and disapprovals or otherwise followed observing prophet's life? Quraan is a revelation to the prophet –the word of God and absolute truth, but not what all in shariah. As far as obtaining Allah's grace is concerned, theoretically speaking, following what is in Quraan should be sufficient. If anything what prophet has said is being followed it is out of peoples reverence to him. Two most popular are Hadith of Muhammad ibn Ismail aL -Bukhari and Muslim ibn al-Hijjaj al Qushayri.

Ayesha's marriage—Though many are not so particular to comment on other wives of Prophet married after Khadija's death, there are many to discuss the Prophet's marriage with Ayesha. She was only 9/10 years at the time of marriage and Prophet was very old-53 years. (**Self-**Child marriages were common even in Hindu civilisation both with and without a wide gap between the partners. Even today many child marriages take place though not with so much of age gap between the partners as in the olden days. However, one major difference between child marriages in the ancient times and modern times is, the girl is married only after attaining puberty and not before. It is difficult to speculate about Ayesha regarding her puberty status. She may or may not have not attained puberty at the time of marriage. In the present times it is believed that puberty occurs in girls between the ages of 10 and 14. Between 12 to 14 is more common. Further present day scientists say that the age of onset of puberty has considerably decreased over a period of time. Hence, any puberty at 10 yrs or below is considered as a precocious puberty and can also result in pregnancy in smaller number of cases compared to the average. The problem of child marriages was so severe in India that the British agreeing to the views of social reformers has passed a Child Marriage Restraint Act-1929, which came into effect from April 1,1930 and it was applicable to all of British India and not just to Hindus. The act is popularly known as the Sharda Act. The act fixed the age of marriage for girls at 14 years and boys at 18 years which was later amended to 18 for girls and 21 for boys. However, even today debates are going in the country as to why there should be different age limits for boys and girls ? Because, India at one point of time reduced the age limit for voting to 18 yrs for both the genders. So when a person can vote he also has the right to marry. Not yet legally approved. There are two questions that arise of which one is more serious tantamount to crime. When a girl is married before puberty and continue to remain with the husband, there are no specific commands given to the husband. Is it right to involve with the girl before she attains puberty ? Is he prohibited to involve or not ? If prohibited but get involved any punishment prescribed ? The second question is, as per the modern Doctors the age of even normal puberty is not the recommended age for giving birth. The girls have to wait for some more years. However, it was not possible for ages and even now no law could prescribe anything regarding this issue. In the modern times not only in the highly developed west even in India legal debates are there about a situation called “Marital Rape”. Rape is a serious offense in Islam and the Punishment is severe. Now the question is, suppose a wife refuses, can a husband force on her ? Does it tantamount to rape ? No such issue raised in Islam. In USA, it is illegal and punishable. In India, there is a strong support to make such an act as illegal. We do not know how Islam views it.).

Prophet’s succession—Though Allah has chosen Muhammad to become Prophet but Allah was not merciful at all to him with respect to his children. Allah has snatched away all of them prematurely and Ayesha who preached Quraan for a long time after the death of Prophet Muhammad, was not blessed with any child and Prophet Muhammad was very unfortunate to see all his children die while he was alive except Fatima. Fatima also died a few months after the death of prophet. Hence prophet was deprived of nominating anyone of his sons as a successor. Apparently he left without giving definite instructions regarding his successor. That would have probably avoided divisions in Islam.

The leaders of both Sunnis and Shias are closely related to Prophet. Abu Bakr was only a companion who later became Prophet’s father in law. Ali was the cousin and son-in-law of prophet. So blood-wise Ali is close to Prophet than Abu Bakr. (**Self**-However, many of different affiliations, were/are of the opinion that in case of religious matters dynasty/ blood closeness need not or should not form the basis of succession. Spiritual inheritance is different from descent by blood. The successor must be spiritually a competent man as close in calibre to the initial person. Such a person has to be selected for the proper continuity). Prophet is supposed to be related to all the four Caliphs. So it is natural for every one of the four to claim something which leads to factions.

Chapter - 5

(A) Forbidden Foods—2:173; 16 :115; 6: 121 and 131 to 146; 5:3 and 4;—The following foods are forbidden to eat. Dead meat (decaying flesh of dead animals), blood, swine (pig) flesh and any animal which has been invoked and immolated in the name of any God other than Allah. However, a condonation is given. Those who are driven by necessity, neither craving nor transgressing, it is no sin for them to eat the above. Allah is forgiving and Merciful. Similarly it is told in **5 : 3**. "Whoso is forced by hunger, not by will to sin, for them Allah is forgiving and Merciful". This condonation is very essential particularly in poor negro countries and for poor people in other countries. Can Muslims eat pig meat? The above is the answer. In the above surahs what and which animals are permitted is also given.

During pilgrimage it is prohibited to hunt and eat on land. But if you are travelling by sea then one can hunt in sea and eat fish of the sea- **5 : 96**. (**Self**- While only fish has been mentioned maybe it covers other edible sea food as well).

Though Judaism and Christianity are classified as Abrahamic religions, barring a minority, all Christians eat pork and a large majority of Jews eat pork particularly in USA. Apart from the above mentioned religions in other parts of the globe, pork is eaten by so many religious/ social groups. In fact, negroes and several other across the globe were traditionally eating pork before getting converted to Islam.

Camel though it is permitted it is not here in all regions. So the culture of eating camel's meat was/is not there in such places. Similarly if sea is not there at any given place the question eating seafood does not arise.

(B) Usury—Money lending on interest and thereby making money is prohibited and is considered as a sin (**2: 275; 2:276;**

3: 130). Since long it is known in India (maybe in other countries too) that Afghan Pathaans do money lending and they do not consider it as wrong apparently. They are known for money lending. It is so with some other Muslims in different countries. In the present times people keep money in government banks and the Governments themselves give interest in proportion to the money saved. It is considered as perfectly legal. And governments in turn gives loans to people on interest. Of course there are also banks which can charge money for the maintenance of your money saved in their banks.

(C) Hoarding of Gold and Silver is prohibited (9: 34 and 9: 35). This seems to have been said apparently keeping Jews and Christians. (Hence, it is possible that usury also has been said with respect to Christians and Jews) Maybe they were doing so. And severe punishment for them is mentioned for them on the last day of judgement (Qiyamat). (It is quite possible that idolatory also was being referred to some Christians and Jews besides others. As mentioned above idol worship is not approved as per one of the ten commandments in Bible). (**Self**-Only Gold and silver are mentioned. Other precious items like diamonds, pearls etc are not mentioned. Probably they were not so popular in prophet's time. In the present times I do not think the above stipulation is followed by the people. Those who are rich, they purchase lot of jewellery, silver, diamonds, pearls etc and keep at home. For women they are ornaments and even men also want to see them bedecked in jewellery. Even men wear some jewellery items. Now-a-days we have even platinum jewellery. Even otherwise they can hoard Gold in the form of bars, biscuits etc. In Gulf countries many are rich and are very likely to have the above items. Further in the present times Gold is the standard for international transactions. So lot of Gold is stored by the respective governments and this is under the control of the Prince/King/dictator or under the control of various officials in a democratic form of government.

(D) Adultery—Forbidden and serious punishment (**17:32; 24: 2 to 9**)–Adultery is punished by one hundred lashes/flogging both male and the female. However there is an obligatory condition. Those who accuse must bring minimum of four witnesses who are believers.

Otherwise the punishment cannot be given. (**Self**—It is difficult to imagine that those who indulge in adultery would be so careless to be witnessed by four people ! They would indulge in a secret manner. It is both carelessness and misfortune that those who indulge are caught by four people and such cases would be rare/very limited. Of course now-a-days it may be more possible. Say if somebody is involved in adultery in a hotel/lodge and somebody comes to know, it may be possible to have witnesses. Further in the present times hotels/ lodges are fixing secret cameras and so if their photos somehow get into circulation then there is no problem of witnesses at all).

Those people who have accused but could not bring four witnesses are punished by eighty lashes. In case the man who accuses his wife of adultery but has no witnesses then he has the following option. He can swear by Allah four times and as a fifth time swearing he should invoke curse of Allah on him if he has falsely accused his wife. Mercifully the same privilege and option is given to females/wives as well. A female/wife can also swear by Allah four times and as a fifth time swearing she should invoke curse of Allah on her if she is telling a lie. In that case she cannot be punished. Suppose both the man and the woman swears as above!? Nothing can be done. In view of **24 :3** one gets a doubt whether those involved in adultery–even proved-should be punished ? Because anyhow a punishment is given to them in the form of restricting their marriage. They cannot marry any one they like. Believers are not allowed to marry them. An adulterer can marry only an adultress or an idolatress and an adultress can marry only an adulterer or an idolator. So when such a restriction has already been imposed it would be benevolent on the part of custodians that they may be exempted from the above punishment with or without some atonements. It all depends on how compassionate the native clergy is.

Suppose a married male is caught involving with an unmarried female, in case the male agrees to accept her as another wife (within the limit of four) and if the lady agrees to become his wife, should they still be punished or may be forgiven ? Of course this possibility is not there for females as a married female cannot marry another man. Suppose the man goes to another country and get involved in adultery, who is there to monitor him? He may be caught or he may not be. It is also not clear whether an involvement with kaafir woman (non-believer women) within their own country or outside their country is treated as adultery or is ignored. It is also not clear about the involvement of a single (unmarried man) with a single (unmarried woman). Suppose they are caught and both agree to marry each other should they still be punished? (Of course this cannot be termed as adultery but involvement before marriage by singles. May be the clergy has answers for the above questions but it is natural that those who are caught pray for kind consideration to the clergy). In other societies the outcome can be of more than one type. They may be forgiven in case they agree to marry each other. Or they may be simply get separated by their parents as they may not be interested in their marriage or one or both of them may be punished. In developed west and other liberated societies involvement by consent is not an offense and is legally and socially approved. No action can be taken. Of course there is a prescribed age limit for the individuals which can vary from one country to another.

In liberated societies adultery may not be a serious issue and at the most it can result in Divorce. And there is no social stigma for such happenings.

(E) Prostitution–Prostitution is banned in Islam. However, though adultery has been discussed in Quraan, no such discussion about prostitution except a mention in one ayat (**24:33**-An-Nur-Light) where it is said "Force not your maids into prostitution when they desire chastity. If they are forced to prostitution Allah will forgive the women". So it means that prostitution was there during prophet's time as well. Secondly, though it is said "Allah forgives the women who are forced" it does not mention any punishment for the men who force the women into prostitution. This has a serious implication for the present times where so many women are forced into prostitution by men. So it is the mandatory duty of the local clergy and other cultural custodians to decide the punishment for the men who force women into prostitution. In the modern form of governments there are some laws but are not enforced strictly. Rather the governments are not really bothered to the extent they should and even conniving.

Sex Industry is a multi-billion dollar industry at the world level and even to some individual countries it is a billion dollar industry contributing significantly to the nation's economy. Some of the money is legal while some is underground economy. Since it can contribute a lot to nation's economy it is encouraged by the local custodians. Prostitution is legal in many countries and is also illegal in many countries—both Islamic and non-Islamic countries. Paradoxically in two Islamic countries, Turkey and Bangladesh, prostitution is declared as legal. But they are very much in the Islam fold without any ostracisation. In Lebanon also where 58 per cent are Muslims prostitution is legal). (Before Bangladesh and Pakistan got separated from the rest of India in both the regions prostitution was there. Now only Bangladesh has declared it legal, though not Pakistan.).

The general opinion prevailing in the world is, though prostitution is illegal in many countries, it is an open secret that prostitution occurs in a large way and is widely tolerated. So it is obvious that local law enforcing custodians actively connive. Where it is legal also prostitutes are exploited by middlemen, muscle men and law enforcing agencies highly depriving the prostitutes of their earnings. Similarly is the situation where prostitution is declared as illegal but is allowed by connivance of local custodians. A pitiable state indeed. No one should be in such a bad economic state so as to enter into prostitution for their survival. All the rich nations have a moral responsibility in this regard at least to those whom they consider as their fellow women. In some countries where prostitution is legal, the prostitutes are not the local people but imported women. Local people are well off not to depend on prostitution. Probably in future more and more countries may legalise prostitution for their own reasons.

People can go to other countries where prostitution may not be a problem (men go to indulge and women go to indulge in the profession) and return back as and when they want. Prostitutes may not be locals but imported from various countries. They may be belonging to any religion, any faith etc. Female human trafficking is considered as a serious problem in the world, though exact statistics are not available.

Belief in God or any other supreme force seem to have no correlation with disposition to prostitution. Both theists and atheists/

agnostics may approve/indulge in prostitution and/or believe in high degree of social freedom. Religious restrictions—if encountered–maybe somehow circumvented. Though prostitution is banned in Islam it is not clear whether involving with prostitutes who are non-believers is permitted.

(F) Circumcision—Not mentioned in Quraan and does not seem to be absolutely mandatory. However, Muslims do circumcision for their male babies few days after birth. This practice was there even before Prophet Muhammad was born in many social groups both Arabs and non-Arabs. Some people in many social groups across the world–Muslims and non-Muslims–can be born already circumcised, that is by birth they do not have the foreskin a condition called "aposthetic".

Since Islam spread to many countries and many got converted into Muslims at an adult stage it is quite unlikely that they have undergone circumcision. In olden days, medical science was not so advanced and general anaesthesia was not available. In the present times general anaesthesia is available and so it is possible for adults also to undergo circumcision. But it does not seem to be occurring so to any large extent for adults. Babies however are circumcised.

Though it is universal in Muslims and nearly so in Jews it is not so among Christians. People following New Testament do not give much emphasis on circumcision. In countries like UK–a protestant country–per cent of circumcised people are very less. And in Germany it is banned as it is thought to violate the child's rights. Though all Abrahamic religions do undergo circumcision, in general it may be said that the percentage of circumcision has been steadily declining with time among Christians and the decline is also reported in Jews.

In some pockets of the world female circumcision was/is practiced. That has/is been viewed by many people both males and females that it should not be on females. However, this practice also has considerably decreased. In fact, the way female circumcision is opposed by many males, male circumcision is opposed by many females. Many atheists/agnostics oppose circumcision. Female circumcision also was / is practiced both in Islam and others in many countries. The extent to which it is done may vary across people.

Other names, for female, circumcision are female genital mutilation and female genital cutting. However, neither male circumcision nor female circumcision is mentioned in Quraan.

(G) Veil—According to Karren Armstrong—She might have confirmed from several sources before making this statement. "Quraan does not prescribe veil for all women but only for Muhammad's wives as a mark of their status".

A confusion may arise because of the Ayat **33:59.** Here it is said "O prophet Tell thy wives and thy daughters and the women of the believers to draw their cloaks close around them (when they go abroad). Then they will be recognised and not annoyed. (**Self**-This Ayat can give an impression that the cloak is not only for prophet's wives but also to other women belonging to prophets family—though only daughters are mentioned. The words in the Ayat "and the women of the believers" is confusing. Whether the addressing is confined to the women of Prophet's family or to all women? If the stipulation is meant for all women then there is no need for specifying prophet's wives and daughters. It could have been simply said that all believers should draw their cloaks. So as Karren Armstrong said, the veil is at the most for the women of Prophet's family. But the Ayat also seem to say that the cloak is not compulsory even for prophet's family always but is so only "when the women go abroad" i.e. to other countries or at the most one may infer "much away from their residential places.

In no translation of Quraan the word Hijaab or Jilbaab is used. In case it is in the original Arabic ayat, such a key word cannot remain unmentioned, when so many other key Arabic words have been mentioned. Neither any description of the extent of covering of the body is clear from the Quraan. In reality we see extremes. A veil just partially exposing the eyes and women moving freely without any veil. (The English word Cloak probably is not an exact equivalent to a full veil (hijab).

(**Self**—In many countries even some predominantly Muslim countries and in countries where a large Muslim population is there not all women, always use Veil. And even when they use they may or may not cover their faces. And they are accommodated by other Muslims and Muslim clergy. No one attacks them by religious custodians in any manner. In Hindus though there is no veil, in the past women were asked to cover their faces while talking to others or talk from behind a curtain. I presume the practice is almost eliminated. In India and maybe in other countries too we have Muslim female actresses acting in cine movies along with men both believers and non-believers. And it is so with male cine actors. As per Islam it is not approved. But Clergy is kind enough in these places.

Similarly, Quraan nowhere prescribes that men should shave off their moustache but keep only their beards. This is evident from the present day Muslims even in Arab countries. This is also evident from the Muslims in other countries. They may keep both moustache and beard, keep only moustache or shave only the moustache and keep the beard or even shave both the moustache and the beard. No clergy is against it. The fact is that you find the above patterns even in Muslim countries and even Arab countries. In India so many Muslim cine actors could not have become so famous and wealthy had they retained their beard and moustache or if they have shaven their moustache and kept only beard. They would not have been selected for the cine movies. In other religions also there are mandatory hair styles. For example, in Sikhism men are supposed to keep both beard and also hair on the head along with a turban. Of course some do not. But predominantly they retain. As mentioned for Muslims some Sikhs could not have become famous cine actors had they retained their hair style. Hindu saints do keep both beard and hair on the head and may grow indefinitely or sometimes trim and sometimes they may completely remove the hair and again start growing hair. In the present days Hindus because of western fashions maintain different hair and beard styles. Often even parents do not like their children to have such fashions but are helpless.)

(H) Rosary—Rosary is not mentioned in Quraan. According to one site on Google, the rosary is used by all classes of Muslims and in all lands today, with the exception of the Wahhabis in Arabia. Christians and Jews also use it. Not only it is used to recite the name (s) of the God but is also worn by many. However, wearing does not seem to be a custom in Muslims. Some wish to differentiate the terms "Prayer Beads" and "Rosary" while some use the term Rosary for Prayer beads as well. The beads are termed "Subha" and "Tasbih" in Urdu and Arabic respectively. In Hindusim the Rosary is called Jap (a) Maala.

Rosary is used in many religions as mentioned above. However, the number of beads, number of beads with different sizes and their arrangement in a rosary may vary across faiths. The material with which beads are made can also vary in the rosary.

In Islam, since 99 names of Allah have been mentioned, there are/have to be 99 beads. As per Hindu methodology of making a rosary in the above case all the 99 beads will be of the same size and continuous with just one bigger bead which acts as an indicator that one round of recitation of all the names is completed. However, it appears that in Islamic rosary the 99 beads are separated into three sets of 33 beads with an indicator/marker bead at the end of each set.

Since the usage of Rosary is not mentioned in Quraan nor in no way authoritatively recommended its usage is apparently varying. It is so in Hinduism too. One may use once in a way or one may not use at all. One can have alternative ways. They just recite all the prescribed names of the God from a printed book. All do not wear nor those who wear, wear it from any prescribed period. The form of the rosary also may vary.

(I) Ensoulment, Abortion and Contraception—In religion, **ensoulment** is the moment at which a human being gains a soul. Since ages there had been a lot of debate in all faiths on the time of entry of soul and whether this time is the same for males and females etc. This debate has a direct bearing on the issue of abortion, whether it is moral or not. If moral up to what stage ? The answers seem to vary across the faiths and even in the same faith from time to time. Answer varies very widely- One extreme is ensoulment happens right at the moment of conception and the other extreme is ensoulment happens when the child takes the first breath after being born. Another common view is anywhere between 40 to 120 days after conception.

In general abortion is strongly discouraged in Islam. In support of this Ayats **6.151** in Darussalam and Saudi Quraans and **6.152** in Pickthall's Quraan and **17 :31** in all the above Quraans are quoted. (However, it is debatable whether they refer unambiguously to abortion).

(**Self**—It appears in Darussalam Quraan translations of **6.151** and **152** of Picthall's Quraan are merged together as evidenced by other points as well). What the above Ayats say is 'Don't kill your children fearing poverty. We shall provide sustenance for them and for you. Killing children is a great sin. The translation of the above Ayats can be confusing. Are they really related to the issue of abortion? "Children" can mean those who are already born and are being reared. So what is considered as a sin is probably killing those who are already born. While abortion refers to those who are not yet born. Only scholars have to make it clear. No doubt in very olden days there could have been some crude methods of inducing abortions. But if done so it would be known and due action can be taken. Secondly, the promise made in the Ayats "We shall provide them sustenance for them and for you" is not true in the present times as many are deprived and this is a matter of common knowledge. All over the world so many children suffer from malnutrition, starvation, poverty and lead a miserable life and even many starvation deaths can occur. And their parents too. So what is really a better choice? Prevention is better than cure. Otherwise there will continue to be a huge population of both children and parents living a miserable life. Many schools of Islam do debate about as to which is a greater sin. It really needs to be seriously reflected.

The wide varieties of opinion of Islamic schools may be listed as follows:

(a) abortion is permitted unconditionally before 40 days;
(b) abortion is permitted unconditionally before 120 days;
(c) abortion is permitted at any time if there is a danger to the mother's health;
(d) abortion is permitted in cases of rape (However, even in cases of rape also the maximum permissible time limit is as above i.e. before 120 days).

In the present days medical science and technology is highly advanced and we have the technique of amniocentesis. This technique is also called as amniotic fluid test or AFT and is used in prenatal diagnosis of chromosomal abnormalities, developmental abnormalities in the developing baby and foetal infections. But this technique is of the recent times and therefore permitting abortions under the above conditions in olden days does not arise. This technique while it is allowed in certain countries it is not allowed in certain others as this technique can also be used for sex determination and in some countries parents may selectively wish to abort babies of a particular gender –in particular female babies or illegitimately conceived babies. But aborting abnormal foetuses is probably justified and parents prefer it. Muslims allowing abortion in case of mothers life is in danger is really a rationale and humane decision. All Muslim denominations seem to have the same opinion. Unfortunately some other religious denominations do not allow abortion under any conditions. They have to go to another country where abortion is permitted. If they cannot go out in time there can be a casualty of both mother and the baby.

In the developed west the problems are minimised and it is up to the women to decide and expert medical advice is available for further course of action.

Though man indulges for a very long time, the fact that the parents are having only one, two or a few children, even in Muslims—both in Islamic countries and non-Islamic countries—clearly indicate that they are following either contraceptives and/or the concept of safe period to avoid pregnancy. But contraceptives also are apparently prohibited in Islam and their sale is banned in some Islamic countries.

(J) Drinks and Gambling (2:219 and 5:90)—This aspect is again debatable. The mentioned ayats say that strong drinks and gambling, both are a sin but (some) utility for men but the sin is greater than their utility. Further the ayats gives an instruction regarding how much money can be spend on drinks and gambling. It is recommended that one spends on the above, only that much amount of money which is in excess. From the above ayats thus it is clear that drinking and gambling are not totally prohibited. It is apparently not mandatory but only recommendatory to abstain from them. The stipulation that "one should spend only that much amount of money which is in excess" can be a variable. That is for different people the amount of money that is in excess can vary a lot. Rich people may have much more money in excess. Does this mean that they can indulge in them a lot? The following quip is recorded in Indian/British history. When a Britisher came across the famous poet of the Indian sub-continent,

Mirza Ghalib and asked him "are you a Muslim"? Ghalib replied "I am half Muslim. I take wine but do not eat pork"! But as per the above interpretation/explanation in Quraan, Ghalib can say he is a Muslim as he must be spending on wine only that which is in excess. Further gender aspect has not been mentioned in the above ayats. The stipulations are only for males or for both males and females?. At the time of prophet it must have been said only for males. But how about in the present times? Even prohibiting drinks for females, how about games of chance/gambling? Should they also be prohibited? Say for example in the present times females purchasing lottery tickets or investing in market shares etc. Only the native clergy has to decide.

How about drinking/liquor in Muslim countries? A summary of the situation prevailing seems to be like this. Though it is banned, it is allowed for non-Muslims—both residents and tourists—and in all diplomatic missions. Purchase is allowed only from licensed hotels and bars and consumption maybe allowed in these licensed hotels and bars or in the privacy of their homes. Drinking in public and drunken driving is not allowed and a minimum age limit for drinking is prescribed. People are allowed to bring a certain minimum quantity of duty free liquor purchased at the airports. In other words sale of duty free liquor is allowed in airports. No clear prescription is mentioned regarding women consuming the liquor. But it is a matter of common knowledge that in diplomatic missions of the developed west and other countries both women and men drink. Apparently even tourists from these countries can also drink in licensed hotels and bars or on in the privacy of their homes. Sale of liquor illegally is not ruled out. In fact, travel agents and tourist operators suitably advise their tourists regarding liquor and night life situation and other Do's and Don't's in different countries. So that they can accordingly plan.

In many countries including the countries of the other two Abrahamic religions drinking is legal and even is a part of culture, and both males and females may drink. Wine can even be an item in some religious functions. Not only clergy consume but even audience attending the church can be served wine on specific occasions. In India the situation is rather variable. While liquor is illegal in some states-rather few-it is legal in most other states. Not only that, even in the same state the situation can vary from time to time. In some states the government itself is running the liquor business and it is allowed in the constitution of the country. In countries like India, Malayasia, Singapore etc where there is a mixture of religions and have a significant Muslim population it is really impossible to monitor and specifically punish a Muslim for liquor drinking. The clergy in these countries knows the state of affairs and are apparently understanding and merciful.

Though not for legal or religious reasons, Government of India has of late started creating an awareness campaign for liquor and tobacco and projecting them as injurious and can be fatal. In several media they give statutory warnings and on the above products by law statutory warnings are mentioned. Doctors have told that nearly 75 per cent of the cancers are due to tobacco and alcohol. Yet the government is not able to ban these. Apart from the above consequences the families are ruined economically and become seriously deprived. So irrespective of any religion or in the absence of any religious prohibition the use of the above should not be there or at least minimised to the extent possible. In fact many people even who indulge in above say emphatically to practice moderation and exercise caution. So the Quraanic prescription of prohibiting/ discouraging liquor is no way offensive to other religions. Rather it is conducive.

Another day-to-day practice which is different in different religions is people entering the places of worship with shoes. It is allowed in many places in churches though not in all. Those who are attending the church with shoes no way feel a sense of blasphemy. So with taking wine in the church. Obviously inner devotion is different from external manifestations. In mosques and temples one cannot enter with shoes. However, exemptions can be given for police and military.

Chapter - 6

A few more points of interest in Quraan

1- (57:20)—Know that life of this world is only play and idle talk, and pageantly and boasting among you and rivalry in respect of wealth and children as the likeness of vegetation after rain, where of the growth is pleasing to the husbands man, but afterward it dried up and thou seest it turning yellow, then it become straw. And in the hereafter there is grievous punishment and (also) forgiveness from Allah and his good pleasure, whereas the life of the world is but matter of illusion.

(Self- These thoughts are of universal appeal. Particularly Hindus would be very happy to listen to the entire Ayat but more particularly the words of the first sentence "Know that life of this world is only play and idle talk" and the last words "whereas the life of the world is but a matter of illusion").

2—(4 :92 and 93)—If you kill a believer (i.e. mumin, a fellow Muslim) he will be in hell for ever. Allah has cursed him and he is doomed. (**Self**—But history has record of wars between believers. We do not know how these situations are interpreted. Apparently some are of the opinion that if a war ensues then the same rules will apply whether the wars are between believers or between believers and non-believers). For a long time people had been telling and even today they tell that lot of blood has been shed in the name of religion. However, a puzzling but a hard fact is, out of the total wars, wars because of religion are far few than wars because of other reasons which are far more. Of the 1763 wars only 123 wars have a religious cause, that is only seven per cent of the total wars in which less than two per cent of the total people killed in all wars were killed. The remaining wars (93 per cent) and the rest of the people killed (98 per cent) were not related to religious causes (Charles Phillips and Alan Axelrod (2012) Encyclopedia of wars—Three volumes—Better world books).

3- -(9:23)—Even if your fathers and brothers are disbelievers (non-Muslims) do not treat them as friends. (**Self-**At least in India this statement has limitations. When India was split into India, Pakistan and Bangladesh, it so happened that some in the same family got converted to Muslims and stayed back in Pakistan and Bangladesh while some could escape or were earlier also staying in India and have not opted to go to Pakistan and Bangladesh. Hence many families had and have close relations. They cannot treat each other as enemies. They are as good. Even in independent India when conversions took place some members of the family got converted and some not. But they remain together more closely compared to those to whom they are not related either by blood or by religion. They dine and wine happily and even prefer to marry. In India yet there is another dimension—of caste—that is a particular social group. (Indian since ages has been divided into numerous social groups whose identity is still maintained even after they have converted to another religion). So people in the same caste/social group may remain together friendly irrespective of the religion to which they belong to. In the same caste/ social group we may have Hindus, Christians, Muslims etc. The same logic as above holds good for Christian converts also in India.

4- Did Allah ever speak to Prophet Muhammad? Yes. **(66 : 3)**-Once prophet told a secret to one of his wives. But she divulged it. Allah told this to Prophet and prophet in turn asked his wife. Wife asked who told him ? Prophet said. It is Allah.

5- (4:17)—Forgiveness is only incumbent on Allah towards those who do evil in ignorance (and) then turn quickly (in repentance) to Allah. From other verses it is understood that the forgiveness is subjected to the condition that the person undergoes atonements as prescribed.

6- Our Life span is fixed by the Allah (**3: 145**). But it is a matter of common knowledge that people die at various ages—starting from still born till 100 plus. So it varies widely with individuals. The answer for this known only to Allaha. In biblical times people used to live for very long compared to the present times. Islam acknowledges it.

Hinduism also believes in people living for unusually long time. Present day rationalists feel that their concept of calculation of time was probably different.

7- (4:90)—If somebody cannot fight but ask for peace, leave them and do not fight. Had Allah willed them to fight he would have given them power. Allah has not willed. Therefore let them go. (**Self-** Obviously those who seek peace should not be killed nor otherwise be forced to do anything in any way).

8- Atonements/Expiations/Compensations/ Exemptions have been prescribed for many omissions both unintentional and intentional (deliberate). Mostly for the former. What other omissions can be forgiven by undergoing atonements only the contemporary custodians have to decide compassionately. Where atonements are prescribed they usually involve, feeding of a specified number of poor people as per one's status, giving cloths to a specified number of poor people, freeing a slave(s) (here there is a confusion whether the slave to be freed has to be a believer or a non-believer. or any one of them or it depends on the type of omission), keeping fast for a specified number of days etc. (**Self**—It is quite possible that if a person feels that he can easily afford the prescribed atonements, then he can commit an omission intentionally. What one can do ? Only on the last day of judgment he may/ will be punished. In fact atonements are prescribed as mentioned above both for intentional and unintentional omissions. For example, atonements are prescribed for deliberately breaking a promise (**6: 89**). So it is sanctioned by Quraan. But breaking a deliberate promise may cause harm to others concerned. But no compensation is prescribed for those who are actually affected because of the deliberate breaking of a promise by a person. This point needs to be reflected. The unintentional omission can even be killing another person and atonements are prescribed for this. Very strangely for intentionally killing a person also atonements are prescribed. Hence persons can easily take advantage of this stipulation. Really a serious issue. And this point needs to be seriously reflected. In how many other cases atonements are/can be permitted for deliberately making omissions only the scholars/cultural custodians have to tell. Theft is one such omission that can be considered compassionately in view of the above. Of course it is said in many places that Allah knows what is concealed in your hearts and your intentions. However, the atonements and/or punishments in this world are administered by the native custodians. So the persons are at their mercy). In the present times where modern forms of governments are there, the governments form a constitution for their countries–keeping in view their state of affairs—by framing laws by the duly elected representatives of the people. The constitution tells which omissions are to be punished and how and thus the role of religion is minimised.

9- Those who want to be at peace with you, you should not wage war against them (Such situations discussed in the text elsewhere).

10- Though the virtue of earning righteously can be inferred from Quraan, the topic of corruption—a great evil of the present times—has not been discussed except for one ayat **2:188** where it is said not to confiscate others property by **bribing** the judges. Who were the judges then ? It is not like the present day judiciary. Apparently it refers to clergy who are at the helm of affairs giving judgments. On the whole it appears this evil–Corruption—was not in such great proportions as in the present times. Now the corruption has pervaded all sectors. United Nations after an analysis of the world said "Corruption and Population are the twin evils of the developing world". It also said that "Corruption is AIDS of democracy". Apparently all people from all religions are involved in corruption. As the topic is not discussed in Quraan there is no punishment specifically prescribed for corruption. For corruption it is only the present clergy which has to decide the punishment. And in countries adopting modern forms of government the law enforcing agencies must be vigilant and uncompromising.

11- Quraan repeatedly emphasises not to worship lower deities—Angels, Spirits, Devils (but only expects them to believe in their existence)—and not to treat them as equal to supreme/ Allah. Perfectly fine. No other religion also equals the supreme with lower deities but they are worshipped either for petty gains or for some other reasons. And Quraan apparently acknowledges that Devils can be useful for worshippers. It should be so with other lower deities too 112 (Al-Ikhlas-The Unity and **2:165**). Hinduism since ages believe in worshipping lower deities/evil spirits for small gains. But it is not recommended and the person doing so is likely to meet a sad end. However, to some extent both in Christianity and Islam worshipping lower deities is there and they also believe in exorcism.

12- Though it has been mentioned in the beginning of the text, it is worth mentioning once again the following **highly magnanimous and merciful condonations given by Allah/Prophet to the people--"Allah puts no burden on any person beyond what He has given him." "Allah does not impose on any soul duties and responsibilities beyond its ability to bear them". "Allah desireth your ease. HE desireth not hardship for you" "Allah tasketh not a soul beyond its scope".**

In view of the above it is the duty of all of us to assess honestly every one individually for their omissions and then only react to the person.

General remarks—

1. **How to grow spiritually?/Can we all grow spiritually in the same manner in all times and in all circumstances?**

(a) One may have to agree with Karren Armstrong. One should give credence to her views as she remained both as a nun and also a scholar of comparative religion and philosophy. She is of the opinion that the same conception of God/ divine may not work for everyone. A cryptic summary of Karren Armstrong is, people can grow spiritually in different ways. No single method can contribute equally to the spiritual growth of all the people in the world. And there is a need for the spiritual growth of every one. Hence there should be freedom to chose the path or method.(**Self**-As Indian philosopher Swami Vivekananda said: "Each soul is potentially divine. The goal is to manifest this divinity by controlling nature, external and internal. Do this either by work, or worship, or psychic control, or philosophy-by one, or more, or all of these-and be free. This is the whole of religion. Doctrines, or dogmas, or rituals, or books, or temples, or forms, are but secondary details." So one has/should have a wide option to choose. This freedom has to be ensured. All religions put together or even a single religion like Hinduism is like a grand buffet.

One should have the freedom to choose the items and the quantity (extent). It should be so in spiritual growth also as the old Hindu saying "let noble thoughts come to us from every side"). Growing spiritually and ensuring blessings of the supreme is the foremost criteria. Accordingly the conduct. Other details are by inference are of secondary significance. One should distinguish between what is trivial and what is positively contributes to attain the grace of the Almighty.

(b) Ideology developed in different places and at different times depended on the prevailing social conditions. By extrapolation it will change in future too if the social conditions change. Rather the word "social" needs to be expanded as –Social, economical and political conditions.

(c) In the society people are of varying calibre and temperament. So it is only natural that different people follow God in different ways, if freedom to practice religion is there. Not everyone can receive a revelation nor listen to divine voices or witness any interaction with God in any manner. So almost all the rest choose their own ways or combination of and they may be allowed to do so. They should not be oppressed nor treated inferior. It is their devotion that matters and the supreme is all Knower and all Merciful. As often mentioned in Quraan "Allah knows what is concealed in your hearts". So Allah accordingly blesses the persons. Even among the elevated souls there seem to be differences. Sufis experience is different from that of Prophet and with many saints of Hinduism and Guru Nanak of Sikhism, Kabir, Radhasaomi satsangh or Budha of Buddhism or Mahavira of Jainism etc. This where it is worth repeating the ancient Hindu sayings. 'Let Nobel thoughts come to us from every side'—irrespective of any religion or faith. " Ekam Sat Vipra Bahuda vadanthi" which means truth/supreme is one but great souls have told about that in different ways. As to why they did so one has to reflect and follow accordingly.

2. Hindus and for that matter all other religions and faiths believes in the following which Islam says (the terminology, process and the way of expression may differ).

(a) God exists (addressed differently both within a language and across languages).

(b) Creation, Maintenance and final Dissolution are his powers and prerogative. (**Self**-Hinduism symbolically designated three different forms for these three different functions. However, elevated souls and rationalist theists believe in a single supreme power carrying out all the above functions.).

3. Other aspects which Quraan strongly emphasises Viz; due care for the poor, orphans, needy, being kind to parents and kindred, charity etc is whole heartedly acknowledged by all religions and even by atheists/agnostics. They are of universal applicability. Similarly the merciful condonations of Allah mentioned above will be whole heartedly accepted by all. In fact in the modern times we have many welfare programmes for the above both locally and internationally. In fact one of the popular sayings of Hinduism is Jan Seva, Janardhan Seva/Nar Seva Naarayan Seva/Maanav Seva is Maadhav Seva, meaning Service to mankind is service to God/Supreme. "sarvey jana sukhinobhavantu". Let all live in peace. So the supreme takes into account one's other virtues also. It is not just the time and acts devoted to Him exclusively.

Albert Einstein happened to say "Science without religion is lame, religion without science is blind". Einstein was a Jew but the above quote apparently he made for all and not confined to Judaism. So it is not religion *per se* but what you follow in the name of religion. That is what matters.

4. There are many issues of Bioethics (ethics concerned with the modern techniques of Biology) where clergy of all religions intervene. Once revered Pope (not the present one) was condemning the technology of human cloning which was being speculated by scientists as man playing God etc. (of course it is a long way to go to achieve it, if at all scientists can). One scientist made an intelligent reply to the Pope. "Revered Sir, why do you condemn it? Who gave this knowledge of human cloning to us /man? It is God who gave. So it need not be condemned and we are going ahead as per the God's will. The other way of arguing is, man is abusing his free will. Does really man has free will? If so to what extent? Does every man has free will to the same extent? Predestination/fate versus free will is a perennial debate. There is no definite answer neither in Islam nor in any other religion. But theists believe that everything has to be finally approved by the supreme to come into effect.

5. According to Karren Armstrong, Atheism started in seventeenth century. Advances in science and technology and education is one of the reasons. Future advancements can lead to more number of atheists. In fact it is projected that the population of atheists is further going to increase in future (may not be in Islam but in other religions/faiths) irrespective of the further advances in science and technology. It is sufficient if the present state of science and technology reaches all places and people get educated and financially well off. Of course this can also make one a rational or balanced theist as well. Even this happening is most welcome.

6. People look for ideas of religion and philosophy that suits to their contemporary times and the near future at the most. And with every generation some slight change may occur. People do not want rules and regulations either of religion or of the modern day constitutions which interfere with their happiness and security. People want social, academic and intellectual freedom. They do not want anything to interfere with these. Accordingly they function and try to follow religion.

In spite of all the atheism and peoples desire not to follow what is their in respective religions *in toto,* many will still continue to believe in a supreme because nothing else can answer the existence of this universe and various happenings in this universe. Even a million Stephen Hawkings cannot eliminate the concept of a superpower existing.

7. If a study of all religions and faiths of the world is made there will be no more scope to think of anything new. All views and approaches are likely to be exhausted. So what is required for future is for selected committed people to come together and make a study of comparative religion and make a list of points of universal applicability. In fact the Indian philosopher and Late former President of India Dr. S. Radhakrishnan said. “Religions should be cured of their provinciality and must be made to reveal their universality”. For example, Quraanic virtues of “due care for the poor, orphans, needy, being kind to parents and kindred, charity, living by righteous earning etc". Then we can have a uniform code—not entirely—but of core ideologies which can lead us to live together amicably. To some extent points of provincial relevance may not be ruled out and may be accommodated as the world is heterogeneous in terms of so many parameters. Religion is still necessary to prevent chaos and self-destruction in the world. However, it is necessary that religion is so made taking care of the changing realities, human needs of all categories and learning from the past. So as many said religion cannot be 100 per cent the same forever and for all on the globe.).

8. Many religions talk of heaven/paradise and hell. The genesis of old testament mentions creation of heaven but not of hell. There are many both among theists and atheists who deny and express the same opinion. That is they feel that heaven and hell have been created to instil fear among men for not doing wrong things and as an incentive for doing good things. Swami Vivekananda of Hindu religion also said so. Another question that arises is, as per Genesis of Old Testament God created heaven and earth. So before creating the heaven and earth where was God residing? Is that place also called heaven? If so a distinction should be made. Prophet ascended to heaven (Shab-e-Miraj). Is this heaven the same as the heaven created by the Lord in Genesis or different? Apparently seems to be different. Probably the heaven which Lord created in Genesis is for the people after the last day of judgement (Qiyamat). (However, keep in mind the above mentioned views about heaven and hell also) As mentioned in the text religion is not a strong deterrent for doing any crime as there is no fear of immediate consequences on this earth. Because persons may escape punishment here and they will be punished only on the last day of judgement. So religion may not act as a strong deterrent for doing any crime. Similarly so in Hinduism. One will be punished but not necessarily in this birth but in the subsequent births as Hinduism believes in multiple births. The above logic holds good for rewarding persons also both in Islam and Hinduism. Though Hindus believe in multiple births, the mandate is to function in such a way that one avoids multiple births and the present birth be the last one. So one should get liberated and reach God right after the present birth. In that case for a Hindu also it is only one birth.

Though I have made my sublime intentions clear in the preface, I wish to reiterate that I had been no way tried to be offensive or blasphemous and the primary aim of the text is to satisfy the curiosity of a wide range of audience–from beginners to qualified academicians from different affiliations—who can then work for Universal Peace and Harmony. I sincerely request the kind understanding and cooperation of the readers.

Index

G

H

I

J

Q

R

S